SUSAN SONTAG

Susan Sontag

MIND AS PASSION

Liam Kennedy

Manchester University Press

Manchester and New York

distributed exclusively in the USA and Canada by St. Martin's Press

Copyright © Liam Kennedy 1995

Published by Manchester University Press
Oxford Road, Manchester M13 9NR, UK
and Room 400, 175 Fifth Avenue, New York, NY 10010, USA

Distributed exclusively in the USA and Canada
by St. Martin's Press, Inc. 175 Fifth Avenue, New York, NY 10010, USA

British Library Cataloguing-in-Publication Data
A catalogue record is available from the British Library

Library of Congress Cataloging-in-Publication Data
Kennedy, Liam, 1961-
    Susan Sontag : mind as passion / Liam Kennedy
      p. c.m.
    ISBN 0-7190-3785-9. — ISBN 0-7190-3786-7 (pbk.)
      1. Sontag, Susan, 1933- —Criticism and interpretation.
    2. United States—Intellectual life—20th century. I. Title.
    PS3569.O6547275 1995
    818'5409—dc20   95-911
                                        CIP

ISBN 0 7190 3785 9 *hardback*
ISBN 0 7190 3786 7 *paperback*

First published 1995
99 98 97 96 95   10 9 8 7 6 5 4 3 2 1

Typeset in Aldus
by Koinonia, Manchester
Printed in Great Britain
by Biddles Ltd, Guildford and King's Lynn

CONTENTS

ACKNOWLEDGEMENTS

My thanks to Richard King, Douglas Tallack, Richard Godden, Katharine Reeve, Vanessa Graham, Mick Gidley, Brian Harding, Mark Jancovich, and Stephen Shapiro.

I am grateful to Birmingham University for the study leave and grant that enabled me to bring this project near completion.

This book is for Sharon and Nathan.

ABBREVIATIONS

For books frequently cited, the following abbreviations are used

The Benefactor (London, 1983; first published 1963)	B
Against Interpretation (New York, 1982; 1966)	AI
Death Kit (London, 1967)	DK
Styles of Radical Will (New York, 1987; 1969)	SRW
On Photography (London, 1979; 1977)	OP
Illness as Metaphor (Harmondsworth, 1983; 1978)	IM
I, etcetera (New York, 1979; 1978)	IE
Under the Sign of Saturn (London, 1983; 1980)	USS
A Susan Sontag Reader (Harmondsworth, 1983; 1982)	SSR
AIDS and Its Metaphors (London, 1989)	AIDS
The Volcano Lover (London, 1993; 1992)	VL

Introduction

REASONING IN PUBLIC

W RITING in 1969, *Partisan Review* editor William Phillips observed:

> More than any other writer today, Susan Sontag has suffered
> from bad criticism and good publicity. If she could be rescued
> from all her culture-hungry interpreters, it might be possible
> to find the writer who has been made into a symbol. This is no
> longer easy because a popular conception of her has been
> rigged before a natural one could develop – like a premature
> legend.[1]

Not much has changed in the last twenty-five years in so far as
Sontag's name would still seem to carry with it explicit intellectual,
cultural, and political connotations for many. 'The standard picture'
in the late 1960s, Phillips noted, 'is that of the up-to-date radical, a
stand-in for everything advanced, extreme and outrageous'.[2] The
picture has taken on some new shadings over the years, but whatever the reworkings of this popular conception, all testify to the
teasing implication in Phillips's comments: if Sontag did not exist
American intellectual culture would have had to invent her. In a
sense it has invented her. Sontag has been made into not one, but
many symbols: 'The Evangelist of the New', 'Miss Camp', 'The Dark
Lady of American Letters and 'The Last Intellectual'. Sontag's
intellectual role and contribution to American cultural criticism
cannot be easily prised apart from such popular conceptions. Probably the most widely read intellectual of her generation, her critical
trajectory from the early 1960s to today has been a highly public
one.

When Sontag arrived on the New York intellectual scene in the
early 1960s it was a time when American intellectual culture was

ripe for change. The early essays, collected in *Against Interpretation* (1966), polemically stated her avant-gardist tastes and mocked the parochialism of American arts and criticism, offering to recast intellectual agendas. Sontag seemed to catch, even to lead the new American wave, a 'new sensibility' in her own phrase, which swept much before it. Submitted to a media exposure hitherto rare in American intellectual life she took on an iconic significance within the context of rapid cultural changes and radicalisation – she has since found it difficult to shake off her association with 'the Sixties'. Although she began in the 1970s to self-consciously distance herself from the avant-gardist and radical labels, her visibility as a public intellectual has remained high. Her writings on photography and on the metaphorisation of illness have been widely read and discussed, while her political views – on the Vietnam War, on Cuba, on the American left and communism, on human rights and freedom of expression, and on Western responses to the wars in Yugoslavia – have proved every bit as controversial as her cultural criticism and drawn considerable media attention. The 'standard picture' of Sontag in recent years is no longer that of the up-to-date radical, though the aura of the *enfant terrible* remains, as she is now more likely to be imaged as an inimitable figure of formidable intellect and powerful advocate of the 'high' arts – one of the last of a kind, and no less a legend.

Good publicity allied with the avant-gardist tag has led to Sontag being widely viewed as a 'pop' intellectual; according to Stanley Aronowitz she 'has become the major American example of the Critic as Star'.³ Sontag's response to this view has been to consistently reject and scorn it, insisting on her privacy and distaste for media celebrity. This can seem surprising. With her picture on the front cover of *Vanity Fair*, *Harper's*, and *The New York Times Magazine* and with lengthy, if infrequent, interviews on television, she has hardly been a cloistered cleric of letters. And yet, from her earliest interviews to the most recent she has challenged the imagery of pop celebrity. In a 1968 interview she stresses that her idea of the intellectual life is one of solitude, a life that is 'reserved and contemplative'.⁴ In a 1989 interview she comments:

> Think of the things that I don't do. I don't appear on television. I don't write for any newspaper or magazine regularly. I'm not a journalist. I'm not a critic. I'm not a university teacher. I don't speak out on most public issues. If I wanted to play a pundit role, I would be doing all of these things. Still,

the legend goes on. My life is entirely private. My interests are not those of a pop celebrity.[5]

While it is tempting to view such comments as fallacious reasoning I believe they reflect a significant tension between private and public intellectual demands which is characteristic of Sontag's writings. In her essays and fiction she foregrounds the inwardness of intellectual activity, what she terms the 'private revolutions' of the mind, while seeking to contribute to a wider dialogue of ideas which her writings must enter in order to take on public meaning. To put this another way, there is a strong if submerged autobiographical element in her writings, an intellectual self-examination made public. And so she views her pop celebrity as an affront; her tongue is only partly in her cheek when she tells an interviewer: 'I have a lot of anxiety about being understood.'[6]

It is no easy matter 'to find the writer who has been made into a symbol', for the cultural significance of this writer combines both the *œuvre* and the image, it resides both in the body of writings she has produced, and in the public role she performs. There are many who prefer to focus on the image and argue that the writings lack substance. Greil Marcus, for example, charges that 'Sontag has achieved a presence on the page because she has made herself felt in the media at large'.[7] Such criticisms tend to dismiss what is 'on the page' and so fail to really engage her written contributions to American cultural criticism or even consider the coherence of her intellectual practice, spanning diverse disciplines and activities. In this study I examine the relationship between the self-conscious poetics of Sontag's thinking and the objective conditions contextualising it. It is not my aim to save Sontag from her critics, but to illuminate how her work is shaped by a very deliberately conceived and theorised intellectual project, to critically analyse the development of this project in her contributions to major cultural debates, and to situate her work within a wider critical history of the changing conceptions and conditions of public intellectual life in the United States.

From Hollywood High to *Partisan Review*

If there is an intellectual role Sontag has self-consciously performed it is that of the generalist or 'writer-intellectual'.[8] Her free-ranging studies of thought and culture are not the work of a systematic theorist and are clearly marked by personal taste and response. Her essay subjects are strikingly diverse, including essays on happenings, camp, science-fiction films, pornographic literature, photography, fascist aesthetics, cancer, and AIDS. She has explicitly endorsed the generalist model, acknowledging influences, both American – Paul Goodman and Harold Rosenberg, and European – Walter Benjamin and Roland Barthes. In her 1966 introduction to the American edition of Barthes's *Writing Degree Zero*, she asserts: 'Only if the ideal of criticism is enlarged to take in a wide variety of discourse, both theoretical and descriptive, about culture, language and contemporary consciousness, can Barthes plausibly be called a critic.'[9] For Sontag, intellectual generalism requires this widened conception of 'criticism'; it is an ideal of criticism she believes is best met by the writer–intellectual who eschews critical schools and specialisation, working on the assumption that 'no position should be a comfortable one or should be easily held' (*SSR* 346). Sontag's notion of generalism is at one with an insistence upon autonomy, and in this she endorses one of the most prevalent (though increasingly questioned) twentieth-century conceptions of what an intellectual is: a free-floating commentator on the general culture, unafilliated to specific interest groups or institutions.

'The deepest structure in the culture and ideology of intellectuals', comments Alvin Gouldner, 'is their pride in their own autonomy.'[10] In her writings and interviews Sontag evinces such a pride, revealing a strong self-conception of her role as an independent thinker and champion of critical intelligence. It is a role she frequently romanticises, often imagining it as a condition of intellectual 'exile' – the figure of the itinerant polymath recurs in her writings – and the prerogative of the 'amateur' unhindered by disciplinary or professional alignments. Her construction of this intellectual self-image is crucial to an understanding of her work.

'I think of myself as self-created', Sontag has remarked to an interviewer, 'that's my working illusion.'[11] It appears to be a long-held illusion, one that emerged in what she has described as her 'very solitary and bookish childhood'. Born in New York City on 16 January 1933, she saw little of her parents in her early years as they were busy running a fur business in China. Her father died when she was five and a year later, due to her development of an asthmatic condition, her mother and she moved to the outskirts of Tuscon, Arizona. When she was twelve her mother remarried and they moved to a suburb of Los Angeles. While she has generally been reluctant to write or talk about her childhood, the fragmented comments which have emerged do share an emphasis on her early sense of rootlessness and precocious intellectual appetite. In 'Pilgrimage' (1987), an essay-memoir, she portrays herself at age fourteen living in the Los Angeles suburbs as the 'resident alien' in her family, longing to escape the 'long prison sentence' of childhood and finding that literature was the means of escape.[12] She describes her impassioned desire 'to learn everything': 'In my room I wrote imitation stories and kept real journals; made lists of words to fatten my vocabulary, made lists of all kinds; played conductor to my records; read myself sore-eyed each night.' Having already made a start on the Modern Library while in Tuscon, she now began to develop a strong admiration for European modernism: 'I accumulated gods. What Stravinsky was for music Thomas Mann became for literature.' On reading Mann's *The Magic Mountain*, she writes,

> All of Europe fell into my head – though on condition that I start mourning for it … There on the mountain, characters were ideas and ideas were passions, exactly as I'd always felt … And mild, good-natured, chaste Hans Castorp, Mann's orphaned protagonist, was a hero after my own unprotected heart, not least because he was an orphan and because of the chastity of my own imagination … I recognized his vocation for piety; his portable solitude, lived politely among others; his life of onerous routines (that guardians deem good for you) interspersed with free, passionate conversations – a glorious transposition of my own current agenda.[13]

For Sontag, this was the beginnings of what would be a life-long dedication to the life of the mind.

'Pilgrimage' is a portrait of the intellectual as a young woman, and it is remarkably suggestive of the roots of key themes in Sontag's writings – the isolation and self-sufficiency of intellectual being, the melancholia of high modernism, the appeal of self-transcending passions, the demands of a moral imagination – and of the origins of her illusion of being self-created. It also offers to explain the source and character of the marked impersonality (what many critics have termed the 'coldness') of her writings, when she recollects how 'seething with the desire to express' her feelings she preferred to do so 'by focussing feeling away from myself onto something I admired or felt indignant about'.[14] Such sublimation of feeling is certainly characteristic of her prose style and a mark of the self-consciousness of her essays. However, 'Pilgrimage' is also a very self-conscious text, a carefully crafted memoir, and I am wary of reading it as an interpretative key to Sontag's work. (It is tempting to read it, for example, through a psychoanalytical framework which might construe the elements of fatherlessness, dislocation, and fantasy as foundational drives of her intellectual character.) What I do want to emphasise is that Sontag writes here in order to explain (perhaps, in part, to understand) how the youthful self mothered the adult writer–intellectual.

As a 'working illusion' this idea of self-creation is a potent one in Sontag's writings, though, as we shall see, it often signifies less a form of escapism than of defensiveness in her advocacy of the life of the mind, a need to construct and nourish an inner life which affords an imaginary immunity from the claims of others – the defensiveness of an independent intellectual uncertain about collective responsibilities, and the defensiveness of a woman in a predominantly male intellectual world. This working illusion requires a more critical and ideological examination than Sontag is prepared to provide, for it invites us to view her (her self-consciousness notwithstanding) as a maverick intellectual figure, swayed by little more than her tastes and prejudices. I want to argue, on the contrary, that her ideas and self-conception as an independent intellectual generalist owe a great deal to particular historical and political contexts, and are critically shaped by a specific intellectual culture, that of New York from the 1950s to the present.

Sontag's relation to New York intellectual culture also has an early, imaginary stimulus. In several interviews she has recalled her formative desire to be a part of this culture. In one interview she comments:

> when I was a fifteen-year-old kid at North Hollywood High School, I discovered a newsstand at the corner of Hollywood and Highland that carried literary magazines. I'd never seen a literary magazine before ... I picked up *Partisan Review* and I started to read 'Art and Fortune' by Lionel Trilling; and I just began to tremble with excitement. And from then on, my dream was to grow up, move to New York and write for *Partisan Review*.[15]

This dream became a reality in 1961 when she persuaded William Phillips to let her write a review for his magazine. There are signs that in the years between the genesis and the realisation of the dream it was a strong motivating force, though it must have seemed to her at times that the community she would find lengthy residence in would be an academic one. Sontag entered the University of California at Berkeley at the age of fifteen, but stayed only a year before transferring to the University of Chicago where she responded enthusiastically to its famed set curriculum and enjoyed the freedom of auditing classes in the graduate schools. It was in one of these graduate classes that she met a young lecturer, Philip Rieff, whom she soon married, aged seventeen. In 1952, the year her son David was born, she entered Harvard as a postdoctoral student in philosophy, later graduating with degrees in literature and philosophy though she did not complete her doctoral thesis. In 1957 she won a scholarship to study at Oxford but quickly moved on to the University of Paris where she encountered an intellectual environment she found more stimulating and better suited to her idea of the intellectual life. In 1959, shortly after her return to the United States, she divorced Rieff and moved to New York with David. She found teaching positions in philosophy and religion at several colleges and set about establishing herself as a New York intellectual.

Sontag's idea of an intellectual life was decidedly unacademic; though she taught in temporary positions in New York, mostly at Columbia University, into the late 1960s it was only for as long as she needed the financial support. Her trajectory from Hollywood High to *Partisan Review* features moments of extraordinary determination. She has said of her divorce from Rieff: 'I did have the idea that I'd like to have several lives, and it's very hard to have several lives and then have a husband … somewhere along the line, one has to choose between the Life and the Project.'[16] After nine years in academe she wanted to get the dream back on track. Again, there may be some degree of self-revisionism in such comments, but there is no doubt that in her imagination she was already part of the New York intellectual world, and she was certainly already intimate with the writing habits and arguments of the writers grouped around *Partisan Review*. However, her relationship with this grouping quickly developed into a complexly volatile one of affiliation and repudiation. As she sought to assert her intellectual identity and find an audience by giving voice to her wide range of interests she soon experienced conflicts between her ideals and the realities of intellectual position-taking. If she had at last found her intellectual home, it was an unstable one, riven by generational and ideological conflicts and not a little inhospitable to the emergence of a prodigal daughter.

The New York intellectuals, the focus of numerous studies in recent years, have been widely viewed as the most prominent formation of intellectual talent in mid-twentieth-century America. There is some disagreement on just how cohesive a grouping these intellectuals formed. For some, they were a distinctive community tightly bound by similar experiences and intellectual struggles, most particularly by their responses to communism and later anti-communism, while for others they were a disparate collection of individuals who had little in common other than geography and their passion for contesting each other's claims – an important intellectual formation only after the events and then in the nostalgic minds of their aging members or naive academics envying a milieu they would never know. While the New Yorkers never produced a coherent collective voice, there were distinctive patternings of values and beliefs, and of styles of writing and argument.

In the middle of this century New York intellectual culture was receptive to intellectual generalists – Edmund Wilson, Paul Goodman, and Harold Rosenberg were prominent examples. The literary critics were more numerous – including, most notably, Lionel Trilling, Irving Howe, Mary McCarthy, and Philip Rahv – but they shared with these generalists a desire to exhibit intellectual range and explore diverse contemporary topics in their writings. They were critics who, in Howe's words, 'found a way to pay attention to a particular text and also comment on the larger cultural context in which these texts had appeared'.[17] Most wrote for the moment, a need established in part by the 1930s imbroglio of political sympathies and conflicts and by the demands of small journal publishing. Stylistically, they showed a preference for the essay form to convey their concerns. As Howe observes, they 'develop[ed] a characteristic style of exposition and polemic ... The kind of essay they wrote was likely to be wide-ranging in reference, melding notions about literature and politics ... It is a kind of writing highly self-conscious in mode, with an unashamed bravura and display.'[18] These intellectuals had a strong sense of European cultural models, not merely as a fact of ethnic inheritance (many were of Jewish immigrant background), but of self-chosen dialogue and identity. In the view of Daniel Bell, himself associated with this grouping, they were many of them 'self-invented', keen to play down family origins and stimulated by a 'hunger for culture'.[19] At the very least, European influences nourished the cosmopolitan sense of culture the New Yorkers often articulated.

An admixture of Marxism and modernism has often been seen as the defining dialectic of New York intellectual thinking mid-century, though by the 1950s Freud shows more influence than Marx. This conjunction of ideas and traditions sparked the best of their writings as they sought to come to terms with an American modernity in the postwar period which was in fact fast outpacing their efforts to interpret it, and by the 1960s left them looking like lonely gatekeepers of high culture values (which they had always been in some form). It is often complained that the mid-century New Yorkers, for all the individual brilliance erratically displayed, failed to leave a lasting legacy – unlike the New Critics, for example, they did not issue in a revolution in literary interpretation which could be codified and packaged for younger generations. There is some logic to this complaint as no scholastic or programmatic theories have been passed on, but in their own way, and with more subtlety than has been generally recognised, they did revolutionise the concept and practice of cultural criticism. They gave new meaning to the term 'intellectual' by associating it with the *activity* of critical inquiry as well as the generalism of the cultural critic's approach. This ideal of critical contention and interventionism, seeking an immediate relation to public issues, is well articulated by Harold Rosenberg in his introduction to *The Tradition of the New*: 'If criticism ... waits for aesthetics and history to reassert themselves, it avoids the adventure of playing a part in events.'[20]

Sontag's work owes a great deal to the New York model of the free-floating intellectual: it has significantly influenced her conceptualisations of intellectual generalism and engaged cultural criticism, her presumptions of critical autonomy, and her commitment to the essay form. While deeply influenced by critical and ideological tenets of the postwar generation her writings have also existed in tension with these. The focus of this study is not simply on how she mimics her New York predecessors – she does not – but rather on how she has made their ideas a significant part of her intellectual inheritance while also revising them under the pressure of cultural and political changes and in response to her European influences.

What it means to be modern

While the New York context is crucial to the development of Sontag's public intellectual career, she also lays claim to a European intellectual tradition. There is nothing new in a New York intellectual looking to Europe, often with the sense that the defining intellectual tensions of an age reside there, but few have identified as strongly as Sontag with the ideas and ideals of high European modernism. Her great themes of melancholic self-reflection, self-enervation, and intellectual exile owe much to her admiration for the achievements of individual modernists: the fiction of Kafka, Beckett, and Sarraute, the cinema of Godard, Bergman, and Syberberg, the theatre of Artaud, and the intellectual projects of Benjamin, Cioran, Canetti, and Barthes. Sontag frequently invokes such culture heroes as an imaginative community of intellect and exemplars of a fractured counter-tradition of modernist thought. Her interest in ambitious artistic and intellectual projects reflects in part her fascination with the idea of consciousness *in extremis*. In her formally severe early fictions she explores deracinated or exalted states of consciousness; her characters are often involved in solipsistic acts of 'mental disembowelment'. In many of her essays she explores the idea of 'the artist as exemplary sufferer' and is drawn to the phenomenology of style or temperament in the writers and intellectuals she admires. The 'mind as passion' and the body in pain are key motifs in her writings.

Reading Sontag, certain modernist terms of value emerge: the negative, the transcendent, the transgressive, the authentic, the difficult, the silent. 'The ethical task of the modern writer', she asserts, 'is to be not a creator but a destroyer – a destroyer of shallow inwardness, the consoling notion of the universally human, dilettantish creativity, and empty phrases' (*USS* 131). She views this task with great seriousness, projecting it as a moral correlative of the principle of negation she prizes in modernist thinking. 'All possibility of understanding', she states, 'is rooted in the ability to say no' (*OP* 23). The urge to negate shapes the style as well as the content of her own writings. Her remarkably self-reflexive prose dramatises the activity of mind as an antinomian or dialectical play of ideas and valorises the restlessness of the self-critical intellect. 'In the passion play of thought', she writes, 'the thinker plays the roles of both protagonist and antagonist' (*SRW* 80). When she proclaims that 'thought is a kind of excess', and celebrates the 'dramaturgy of ideas' in the writings of others, she explicitly announces what is clear enough in even a casual reading of her texts: a fascination with the volitions, imperatives, and even imperialism of thinking. It is no accident Sontag should find herself most at home with the essay form, self-consciously manipulating its provisional and performative features, using it to 'try out' ideas. She favours disjunctive forms of argument: aphoristic and epigrammatic modes of critical expression are widely applied in her writings.

While she finds the modernist ethos of negation compelling Sontag also finds its powers and presumptions waning in her own time, attenuated in part due to the very 'success' of modernism as an adversary culture. This lends her perspective on modernist ambitions an undercurrent of pathos and intensifies her sense of writing at 'a late moment in culture' (*SSR* 426). A strong sense of an ending courses through all of her work, at times veering toward the apocalyptic, at others toward the elegiac and melancholic. In a 1967 essay on E. M. Cioran she writes of her 'sense of standing in the ruins of thought and on the verge of the ruins of history and of man himself … More and more, the shrewdest thinkers and artists are precocious archaeologists of these ruins-in-the-making.' (*SRW* 75). The apocalyptic note sounded here tends to give way in her writings of the 1970s and 1980s to melancholy reflectiveness, and these 'ruins' take on a fuller allegorical significance in her perception that 'the nihilistic energies of the modern era make everything a ruin or fragment – and therefore collectible. A world whose past has become (by definition) obsolete, and whose present churns out instant antiques, invites custodians, decoders, and collectors' (*USS* 120). The archaeologist, the custodian, the decoder, the collector – as these figures recur in Sontag's writings (and are joined by others, most notably that of the aesthete) we recognise them as self-projections, dramatis personae in her passion play of thought.

Sontag is both a searching critic and mournful elegist of 'the breakup of modernist culture, or the decline of the new'.¹¹ Her writings explore moral and political consequences of this breakup, searching out its meanings in the most general subjects – such as illness and photography – as well as in specific artistic and intellectual practices. This expansive critical project affirms not only her custodial relationship to modernism (a role in keeping with the traditional concept of the intellectual as a gatekeeper of particular cultural values) but also her self-conception as an independent generalist. While her 'positions' on specific cultural and political issues have shifted a good deal during her public intellectual career, her core (self-centring) assumptions about the autonomy of intellect have remained markedly consistent. Her metasubject, she is fond of saying, is 'what it means to be modern'. This may seem a nebulous concern so stated, yet it defines for Sontag a particular purview on her culture. It is the concern of an intellectual who is sceptical of but not yet prepared to disclaim the enlightened ideals of modernity she has inherited.

Sontag's independent stance has come to seem increasingly anachronistic, even retrograde, in recent years. The ideas of autonomy and responsibility which support the symbolism of the free-floating public intellectual are now frequently questioned, particularly by academic cultural critics. At the same time, this model of independent intellectual activity is more widely viewed as being in terminal decline, overtaken by the pressures of professionalisation which have given rise to a 'New Class' of intellectual specialists – technical experts, policy advisers, and academics.[22] These pressures have had a major impact in restructuring the intellectual field, and the role of the public intellectual has changed greatly in recent years both in its objective functions and in the ideologies supporting it. The New York model of generalist, contestatory critique has not disappeared but it has a diminished influence in relation to the range of different intellectual needs, outlooks, and styles of thought and writing emergent within a public sphere which has become increasingly polycentric.

If reports of the eclipse of the public intellectual are premature they nonetheless draw attention to the 'public' context of critical thinking. Lionel Trilling articulated an assumption shared by many of the mid-century New York intellectuals when he described the public he wrote for as 'the educated class...those people who value their ability to live some part of their lives with serious ideas'.[23] In her continued commitment to the role of the free-floating generalist Sontag would seem to make similar assumptions to Trilling about the transcendent imperatives of intellect and the existence of a broad, educated audience responsive to a rationalising critical voice. Wayne Koestenbaum has observed that 'the project of social criticism' embodied in her career 'assumes a stationary, attentive readership, eager for diagnosis and calm; her voice casts, as its needed reflection, the image of a society willing to be criticised'.[24] This is a keen observation, recognising that Sontag half-assumes and half-imagines her audience. But this is not to say she simply ignores the fragmentation of coherent political and cultural publics in the United States. She has addressed this process in her writings to argue that it makes more necessary than ever a form of critical thinking that promotes 'free speculation' as the ideal discourse of a public liberal culture. And so she generalises, diagnoses, and provokes, and seeks to transcend the claims of specialists or concerned constituencies when writing about a specific subject. The high-minded idealism of her dissenting approach is evident not only in her cultural criticism but also in political activities. In her prominent involvement in international organisations such as PEN (Poets, Playwrights, Editors, Essayists, and Novelists) – responding to issues of human rights, censorship, and freedom of expression – she has championed the role of the writer as a critical conscience of a larger populace.

Sontag's advocacy of critical autonomy has contributed to her distance from certain intellectual constituencies. Among academics there appears to be very limited interest in her writings; although several of her texts are widely taught, there is little debate about her work and certainly no body of comprehensive study surrounding it.[24] This relative silence (consider the academic coverage her French contemporaries have received) is not to be explained away as an objective judgement. I would suggest, rather, that the model of intellectual activity Sontag is taken to represent alienates many academics, and particularly those associated with the academic left. Academics in the humanities and social sciences have learned to become deeply distrustful of the 'universal intellectual' as they have sought to legitimise forms of oppositional critical thinking from within institutional frameworks. In their selective endorsements of adversarial modes of knowledge they are more likely to look to a Michel Foucault, say, rather than to a Susan Sontag to provide theoretical guidance to intellectual activity. This is not simply a question of radical divergence between the generalist and specialist, rather it is a sign of the different aims and ends at work in struggles for intellectual authority within specific public spheres. It is not surprising that academics should look to theoretical models which challenge ideals of universal thinking and education to posit in their place those of local knowledge or cultural pluralism – ideals which relect the specific conditions of their mediated, institutionalised positions.

There is a similar silence about Sontag among feminists. 'As an intelligent woman', she observes, 'you are open to all sorts of stereotypes', and throughout her career her gender has been spotlighted in ways which obfuscate and diminish her intellectual achievements – a famous example is Jonathan Miller's perverse effort to praise her as 'probably the most intelligent woman in America'.[26] However, while Sontag views herself as a feminist she has written very little on the major feminist debates and issues which have come alive during her own public intellectual career. While this in itself may go a long way towards explaining the limited feminist interest in her work there is also a conflict of intellectual models and values to be considered. Angela McRobbie has written an insightful essay which foregrounds her sense of the 'difficulty...in making a case for her [Sontag's] work from the standpoint of feminism. Sontag presents a sexually ambiguous image and has spent most of her writing career looking at works produced by men. What, if any, conclusions can be drawn?'[27] Among her own conclusions McRobbie argues that while 'Sontag's work occupies an uneasy place in the new radical humanities' this is not solely due to the 'distance' from academic concerns she has chosen but also due to blindspots and questionable assumptions in academic cultural criticism. Observing that 'it might be true to say that in many circles she is viewed with suspicion as at best an elitist, Eurocentric aesthete', McRobbie yet proposes 'it is time that Sontag's contribution to cultural analysis was more fully recognised' and argues that her high profile interventions in cultural and political fields beyond the putatively academic 'are not just important but vital'.[28]

McRobbie's essay is a fascinating example of one intellectual making an empathetic, yet critical, effort to understand the work of another whose perceived cultural values are considerably different from her own. She does not view Sontag's 'lack of interest' in feminist debates as a failing: 'It is not so much that this weakens Sontag's work, or that it constitutes some kind of great omission. It represents rather a peculiar and idiosyncratic disavowal.'[29] I believe McRobbie is right about this and Sontag herself has admitted as much in recent years, albeit in an often oblique or coded fashion. The ending of her most recent novel *The Volcano Lover* (1993) offers an interesting commentary on this disavowal when the revolutionary poet Eleonara de Fonseca Pimentel reflects on her political commitments: 'Sometimes I had to forget that I was a woman to accomplish the best of which I was capable. Or I would lie to myself about how complicated it is to be a woman. Thus do all women, including the author of this book' (VL 419). Throughout most of her work Sontag has sought to transcend issues of gender while privileging an idea of the intellectual which has strong male associations. This can be explained in part if we consider the American and European intellectual traditions she identifies with. McRobbie comments on the latter identification to suggest that the 'distance between Sontag's work and the question of gender indicates...the extent to which in high or late European modernism...there was no critical place for women unless they demonstrably transcended gender.

There was no available space to speak as a woman.'[30] I would add that Sontag's identification with the New York intellectuals posed a similar problem, for this grouping was established and maintained as a 'boy's club' (in the popular parlance of insiders), bar the symbolic position of 'The Dark Lady of American Letters' – a position long held by Mary McCarthy and since allotted to Sontag.[31]

Sontag's 'distance' from feminism is also a product of her more general suspicions of collective intellectual enterprises. 'I don't like party lines', she tells an interviewer in 1975, 'They make for intellectual monotony and bad prose' (*SSR* 332). The tension in her work between private reflection and public address signifies a highly self-conscious attention to the contexts in which she writes and speaks. 'There are many intellectual tasks', she observes in the same interview, 'and different levels of discourse ... people who reason in public have – and ought to exercise – options about how many and how complex are the points they want to make. And where, in what form, and to what audience they make them' (*SSR* 332). Sontag has exercised her own options very selectively and self-consciously, with the sense that to 'reason in public' is as much a rhetorical position as a secular vocation. In her admiring portrait of Walter Benjamin she argues: 'It was important for him to keep his many 'positions' open: the theological, the Surrealist/aesthetic, the Communist. One position corrects another; he needed them all' (*USS* 133). Sontag needs all her positions – the aesthete, the moralist, the left-liberal, the modernist – and attempts to keep these open, the better to dramatise and clarify her shifting perspectives on 'what it means to be modern'.

Sontag's intellectual autonomy should be understood as a potent myth which *both* sustains the singular force and style of her work *and* contains this work within specific structures of cultural value. Her self-styled 'amateurism' is identical with her genius, as it has enabled her to bring to questions of culture, politics, and intellect a distinctive form and angle of inquiry which seeks to open up spaces for critical thinking.[32] Sontag should not be negatively defined by her 'distance' from particular intellectual constituencies. In this study I go some way to examining her writings on her own terms, while also locating these terms (her sense of intellectual autonomy and her advocacy of high modernism, in particular) within specific historical and ideological contexts. My aim is not to incorporate Sontag into academic frames of thinking but to indicate the importance of her work to any student (academic or otherwise) of American cultural and intellectual history of the last thirty years.

BEYOND
THE LIBERAL IMAGINATION

In a lengthy article on 'The New York Intellectuals', published in *Commentary* in 1968, Irving Howe charted the history of this group from the 1930s to the 1960s to argue that their influence 'is now reaching an end', opposed, and being replaced by 'a rising younger generation of intellectuals: ambitious, self-assured, at ease with prosperity while conspicuously alienated, unmarred by the traumas of the totalitarian age, bored with memories of defeat, and attracted to the idea of power'. Denouncing 'the political–cultural style ... the new sensibility' of this younger generation, he identifies Sontag as a leading proponent, finding it 'both embodied and celebrated' in 'a publicist able to make brilliant quilts from grandmother's patches'.[1] Howe's acerbic complaint against Sontag is perhaps more revealing of his own generation's critical and political frustrations in the 1960s than an insightful commentary on the 'new sensibility' and Sontag's relation to it. His essay is not without insight, particularly when he assesses the cultural and political impact of postwar intellectual writing, but in the younger generation he can see only a collective act of bad faith: a loss of intellectual and political seriousness, a repudiation of the critical and moral tenets of high modernism, and a betrayal of an intellectual tradition of cultural radicalism. This is to say that he judges Sontag and likeminded intellectuals against an ideal of critical practice which was largely fashioned in and by the immediate postwar period. What he fails to see, or will not allow, is that Sontag does not simply throw off this heritage but very deliberately interrogates it while also building upon it to develop her own form of cultural critique.

The twenty-six essays collected in *Against Interpretation* were written between 1961 and 1965 and cover a wide range of cultural concerns. These include general essays on aesthetics and contemporary culture as well as essays on philosophy, anthropology, literary criticism, film, theatre, religion, and psychoanalysis. These are disparate subjects and there are varying frames of reference and some conflict of argument in the collection, but there is a unity of aim: an effort to identify and argue the merits of a new form of critical understanding which moves beyond the dead ends of 1950s critical inquiry. For many commentators these early essays posited Sontag as a purveyor of radical chic blown by the slightest winds of artistic fashion. But while an important function of the essays is indeed to identify the new this is done in a much more guarded and strategic manner than has generally been recognised. Howe hits on a half-truth when he describes Sontag '[making] brilliant quilts from grandmother's patches', for many of her ideas – on the functions of interpretation, on style, on aestheticism – are hardly new. What is new, though, is the specific conjunction of such ideas in her work and the contemporary relevance she assigns them. In the 'quilt' of *Against Interpretation* there are discernible patterns of idea and argument, and some striking syntheses of diverse critical and aesthetic traditions. In this chapter I pick out what I see as major patterns and relate these to broader transformations of cultural modernism and intellectual inquiry.

Against Interpretation is littered with very deliberately staged provocations. Sontag writes with both a constant awareness of the contexts of American criticism and readership she works within (while many of the essays are on European subject matter, they all appeared in American journals and clearly address an American audience) and a self-consciousness about the rhetorical character of her arguments. Many of the essays specifically address 'critics', asking that they recognise new aesthetic and cultural developments. There are frequent indictments of American cultural and literary criticism as 'provincial' or reactionary in outlook, particularly lacking in understanding of the new French formalism or the new sensibility in American arts. Though she rarely names individual critics or intellectual movements in these provocations they are often identifiable in a coded form if we look closely at the critical terminology and values she calls into question. As we shall see, it is particularly in her efforts to revitalise the concept of the avant-garde and to posit a new intellectual responsiveness to mass culture that Sontag addresses key debates within postwar New York intellectual criticism. In responding to these debates the essays in *Against Interpretation* reveal a thoroughly localised and even agonistic impetus.

Old and new sensibilities

Where Sontag sets out not only to chart but to urge the transformation of cultural modernism in the early 1960s, the postwar intellectuals were more comfortable in seeking to contain modernist energies and meanings in a delimited high culture sphere. The reasons for this are complexly bound up with the significant reorientation of New York intellectual perspectives and values in their widespread rejections of communism. The disillusionment with communism, which began for some in the late 1930s with resentment at Popular Front activities and grew widespread as Stalinist atrocities became evident, left many intellectuals seeking to redefine their relationship to American society in the postwar years. For most, though not all, the move away from communism meant a diminishment of overt political engagement and the development of a new kind of involvement with cultural analysis and aesthetic concerns. Many commentators have pointed to this shift in intellectual focus to argue that it signified a new rapprochement with American society in which intellectuals were happy to forego political dissent. There is a large truth in this, but New York intellectuals did not simply acquiesce to the conservative pressures of the period. What they did do was seek to defend and legitimise what they saw as defining them as intellectuals – their semi-autonomy from dominant institutional interests.

In 1938, following the Moscow Trials, *Partisan Review* editor Philip Rahv pointed out that intellectuals' disillusionment with communism meant a disorienting experience: 'The failure of capitalism had long been assumed, but the failure of communism was a chilling shock and left the intellectual stripped of hope and belief in progress, with only himself and his own talents to rely upon.'[2] It was this deracinated and alienated intellectual whom *Partisan Review* saw as the radical locus for a new cultural projection that rejected political interference and paid tribute to the idea of cultural autonomy. In the 1940s and 1950s the ideal of the 'adversary intellectual' continued to find wide support among New York intellectuals, but became more and more a reflex response to a threatened sense of identity and some confusion about social responsibility. It is necessary to recognise this desire to protect intellectual autonomy if we are to understand the seeming ease and often clear passion with which intellectuals came to promote high culture and even avant-gardism as spheres of artistic 'value' transcending the politics of mass society.

When, in 1952, *Partisan Review* held a famous symposium 'Our Country and Our Culture', it was clear that for most New York contributors the ethic of dissent had congealed into the murky notion of 'critical nonconformism' and that any battles still to be fought would be conducted in the cultural sphere.[3] The cultural battles fought in the postwar years tended to be defensive. The intellectuals 'came too late', as Irving Howe has observed, 'for a direct encounter with new work from the modern masters', and although he finds they did valuable service in bringing that work to life in an American context he holds that this was a 'task of cultural consolidation' that lacked any energising purpose.[4] It was also a form of consolidation in the sense of a holding action, where high modernism (and certain forms of avant-gardism) promised a critical bulwark against the rapidly spreading influence of the mass arts and media. A battle to which many intellectuals pinned their colours was that between modernism and mass culture.

In the 1940s and 1950s the New Yorkers' cultural criticism paid considerable attention to such perceived cultural dichotomies as avant-garde and kitsch, or high culture and mass culture, validating hierarchical vocabularies such as 'highbrow', 'middlebrow', and 'lowbrow', or 'HighCult', 'MidCult', and 'MassCult'. This interest in distinguishing distinct cultural spheres was in part a defensive intellectual response to the impact on cultural production of mass-mediated forms of reproduction, in part a displaced anti-totalitarian concern to defend against an insidious assault on the mind. Clement Greenberg and Dwight Macdonald were the critics who made the most explicit efforts to categorise distinct levels of culture. In his seminal essay 'Avant-Garde and Kitsch', published in *Partisan Review* in 1939, Greenberg offered avant-gardism as a rallying point for disillusioned left intellectuals and artists. Building a series of arguments around these two 'simultaneous cultural phenomena' Greenberg proposed that the avant-garde establish 'a path along which it would be capable to keep culture *moving* in the midst of ideological confusion and violence'; in its 'innocence', complexity, and appeal to 'ultimate values' it resisted ideological or political inflation. Kitsch ('popular and commercial art and literature'), on the other hand, was immediately and effortlessly accessible to all and a sinister cultural force in fostering the insensibility of the masses.[5] In a series of essays from the mid-1940s to the early 1960s Dwight Macdonald, for all his regnant political radicalism, offered a similar message to Greenberg. In his essays he focused on the dissolution of 'High Culture values' faced with the indiscriminatory onslaught of a 'homogenising' mass culture and a parasitic middlebrow culture. In his 1961 essay he envisioned 're-creat[ing] a cultural ... elite as a countermovement to both Masscult and Midcult'.[6]

Greenberg's and Macdonald's efforts to draw clear boundary lines around different levels of culture reflected more general intellectual uncertainties about how to keep alive a sense of modernist 'nonconformism' in an era which was witnessing the pervasive collapse of the tensions between capitalist society and advanced art. Few intellectuals wanted to face the contradictions of championing a modernism which had lost its active and critical potential.[7] The rhetoric of nonconformity was made to serve the new realism of mature reflection – signifying growth from naive radicalism to a complex apprehension of the difficulties of social change – and help define a critical liberal perspective. Lionel Trilling articulated for many the outlook of the liberal intellectual when, in *The Liberal Imagination* (1950), he described 'the job of criticism' as one of 'recall[ing] liberalism to its first essential imagination of variousness and possibility, which implies the awareness of complexity and difficulty'.[8] This was a coded refutation of ideology and instruction to seek a rational (moral) course between extremes of action and belief. To be sure, this was no crude exhortation to forego critical consciousness, and in Trilling's criticism we find an astute dialectical attentiveness to competing values and ideas. It was rather a refinement of critical consciousness drawing on an Arnoldian belief that the best in art and letters would provide the ethical gauge of civic responsibility.

For Sontag, as for many among 'the rising younger generation of intellectuals' Howe denounces in the 1960s, the main impact of the New Yorkers' intellectual activity was the establishment of too rigid models of taste and evaluation and a too severely rational comprehension of the moral functions of art and criticism. The 'new sensibility' which she would pitch in opposition to such activity was already emergent in the 1950s. Throughout the 1950s new artistic and critical energies were pressing hard against the 'success' of modernism to establish alternative models of style, form and criticism. The early 1960s essays gathered in *Against Interpretation* promote the work of Robert Rauschenberg, John Cage, William Burroughs, and other artists active throughout the 1950s, though widely viewed as experimentally tangential to the mainstream of American modernism. These essays also acknowledge the arguments of the cultural criticism of Norman Mailer, Norman O. Brown, and Herbert Marcuse – critics marginally associated with the New York intellectuals. Sontag's efforts to map her own intellectual influences and tastes would prove a partial yet influential guide to the breakup of liberal cultural consensus.

In *Against Interpretation* Sontag announces her departure from key critical ideas and practices of her New York predecessors most clearly in the essays which open and close the volume, 'Against Interpretation' and 'One Culture and the New Sensibility'. The former essay, polemical in tone, argues the merits of a new formalist aesthetic, while the latter essay ranges widely across the contemporary arts scene in America to identify the practices reflecting a new cultural outlook shared by many artists, writers, and intellectuals. Both essays critique dominant critical values and modes of interpretation. In the title essay Sontag explains she is not opposed to interpretation *per se*: 'I don't mean interpretation in the broadest sense, the sense in which Nietzsche (rightly) says, "There are no facts, only interpretations." By interpretation, I mean here a conscious act of the mind which illustrates a certain code, certain "rules" of interpretation' (*AI* 5). What she is 'against' is particular interpretative discourses – especially those of American literary, film, and cultural criticism – which, she believes, too readily apply familiar categories of cultural knowledge in the act of interpretation.

The form of interpretation Sontag announces herself against is one clearly identified with the New York intellectuals. Although she never makes this explicit, it is clear enough when she denounces 'the modern style of interpretation [which] excavates and as it excavates, destroys; it digs "behind" the text, to find a sub-text which is the true one' (*AI* 6) and goes on to lampoon the depth hermeneutics of Marx and Freud, the key critical models for two generations of New York intellectuals. For Sontag, this form of interpretation 'violates art', it 'makes art into an article of use, for arrangement into a mental scheme of categories' (*AI* 10). This line of complaint continues in the new sensibility essay which questions the 'humanist' concerns of critics who view art as 'a vehicle of ideas and moral sentiments' (AI 300). Lionel Trilling is clearly in her sights here and even more directly so when she argues that for a new generation of artists and critics art does not function as 'a criticism of life' in the Arnoldian sense, and goes on to mock traditional genuflexion to 'the pantheon of high culture: truth, beauty and seriousness' (AI 286). There can be no doubt that Sontag very deliberately responds to the New York intellectual context and is well aware of the shock value of such comments. At one point, in questioning the primacy of moral evaluation, she allows herself some wry humour: 'Outraged humanists, please note. There is no need for alarm. A work of art does not cease being a moment in the conscience of mankind, when moral conscience is understood as only one of the functions of consciousness' (AI 300). Here and in several other essays she takes her opportunities to undermine the high culture seriousness and prurience of fellow intellectuals. 'Notes on Camp' offers a famous example, where she remarks that 'one cheats oneself, as a human being, if one has *respect* only for the style of high culture, whatever else one may do or feel on the sly' (AI 287).

'Against Interpretation' is not only an onslaught on established critical practices, it also promotes a new programme for critical activity and in doing so draws heavily on the examples of critical consciousness in the new arts. 'We have an obligation', Sontag proclaims, 'to overthrow any means of defending and justifying art which becomes particularly obtuse or onerous or insensitive to contemporary needs and practice' (AI 5). This is a central claim of these early writings, that criticism has not kept pace with aesthetic and cultural change, that it is out of sync with new artistic practices, and ignorant of the cultural conditions of their emergence. Sontag argues that the new sensibility

> is rooted, as it must be, in *our* experience, experiences which are new in the history of humanity – in extreme social and physical mobility; in the crowdedness of the human scene (both people and material commodities multiplying at a dizzying rate) … and in the pan-cultural perspective on the arts that is possible through the mass reproduction of art objects.
>
> (AI 296)

The 'contemporary needs and practice' she asks criticism to address itself to arise out of a new, creative awareness of the experience of modernity and a positive recognition that 'a new non-literary culture exists today' (*AI* 298). This context, she argues, demands and is already producing a 'cultural alignment' around visual and aural arts with a correspondent decrease in the preeminence of literature. Echoing Marshall McLuhan, she refuses to lament the demise of the printed word as the dominant cultural form of expression and communication and identifies 'the model arts of our time' as 'music, films, dance, architecture, painting, sculpture. The practice of these arts … [is] the locus of the new sensibility' (*AI* 299).

Sontag is drawn to these 'model arts' because they make a direct sensuous appeal to the eye and ear and promise to reinvigorate critical consciousness of the relationship between aesthetic innovation and mass society. In the context of a non-literary culture in which mass reproduction is predominant, she argues, 'what we are getting is not the demise of art, but a transformation of the function of art … Art today is a new kind of instrument, an instrument for modifying consciousness and organizing new modes of sensibility' (*AI* 296). Sontag is here rejecting both the 'two cultures' debate of the 1950s (the distinctions between the artistic and the scientific debated by F. R. Leavis, C. P. Snow, and others) and the divisions of culture into hierarchical levels common among the New York intellectuals. At the end of 'One Culture and the New Sensibility' she implicitly addresses the intellectual fathers:

> it is important to understand that the affection which many *younger artists and intellectuals* feel for the popular arts is not a new philistinism (as has so often been charged) or a species of anti-intellectualism or some kind of abdication from culture … It reflects a new, more open way of looking at the world and at things in the world, our world … The new sensibility is defiantly pluralistic; it is dedicated both to an excruciating seriousness and to fun and wit and nostalgia.
>
> (*AI* 303-4, emphasis added)

In mapping an expanded field of artistic practices she finds many opportunities to rebut cultural assumptions and biases of an older generation of New York intellectuals.

A significant indicator of Sontag's efforts to set herself apart from the older generation is her references to the shortcomings of 'literary intellectuals'; she refers to their ignorance of 'a new non-literary culture', their obsessiveness with differences between 'literary' and 'scientific' cultures, their 'historic antipathy' to industrialisation and its social effects (*AI* 294). She clearly wants to distinguish her own cultural criticism from that of intellectuals who 'cling to literature as the model for creative statement' (*AI* 298). It is notable that of the twenty-six essays in *Against Interpretation* only four deal exclusively with literature or literary criticism. In this she differs from the main body of recognised postwar New York intellectuals, for while they exhibited a generalist thrust they were predominantly literary intellectuals, viewing literature as *the* medium through which to analyse broader contemporary issues. Thomas Bender has been one of the few critics to comment on these intellectuals' limitations in confronting visual and aural culture, finding them 'terribly inexperienced with the culture of the eye and the ear' and suffering from an 'almost puritanical fear of the seductiveness of the aesthetic pleasure' these organs might afford.[9] Sontag evidences no such fears, in part because she is of a new generation more open to diverse cultural experiences and distanced from the culture wars of the postwar period, and also because she immersed herself in the experimental art scene in New York in the early 1960s where complex visual and performance techniques were central. While I argue that she is by no means as optimistic about artistic innovations as the cultural democracy of her new sensibility argument implies, she appeared an original force in the early 1960s in her speculative analysis of an increasingly diversified and synchronically immediate cultural world.

In her challenge to conventionalised categories of critical judgement and taste Sontag was widely read as a reckless libertarian. Irving Howe mocked that she 'has proposed a cheerfully eclectic view ... Now everyone is to do "his thing", high, middle, or low'.[10] But Sontag is far from being the anything-goes pluralist Howe and others cast her as. While the new sensibility essay is deliberately upbeat and antagonistic, its tone and its optimism about a new, playful avant-gardist attitude are not representative of *Against Interpretation* as a whole. Sontag is not lulled into a McLuhanite euphoria for the advent of the electronic media, but she guardedly promotes his views to the extent that they identify how radical changes in technology necessarily affect 'our ways of thinking, feeling, and valuing' (*AI* 299). (In an essay on neo-Marxist criticism she chides its cultural conservatism and ruefully adds: 'It is odd, and disquieting, that such strongly apolitical critics as Marshall McLuhan have got so much better grasp on the texture of contemporary reality' (*AI* 90).) The willed optimism of Sontag's new sensibility thesis is based on her greater pessimism about the social conditions and psychological experience of modernity.

What Sontag wants from the new sensibility is for art to take on what she sees as one of its primary functions now made historically necessary, that of stimulating and 'educating' the senses. Her demand for this lends a further meaning to being 'against interpretation'. 'Today', she declares in her title essay,

> the project of interpretation is largely reactionary, stifling. Like the fumes of the automobile and of heavy industry which befoul the urban atmosphere, the effusion of interpretations of art today poisons our sensibilities. In a culture whose already classic dilemma is the hypertrophy of the intellect at the expense of energy and sensual capacity, interpretation is the revenge of intellect upon art. (*AI* 7)

While highly critical of American models of cultural interpretation, Sontag's animus 'against interpretation' is much wider reaching. As the rather crude industrial metaphor above suggests, 'interpretation' is the name she lends to a more general condition of rational–intellectual excesses. She posits 'interpretation' as a key functional process for an advanced industrial society 'based on excess, on overproduction', where the senses are dulled and human spontaneity is suppressed. The 'sensory experience of the work of art', she argues, should not be taken for granted but respected and nurtured as a possible counterforce to the social annulment of sensuous awareness. If interpretation, as she insists, is '*the* modern way of understanding something, and is applied to works of every quality', then the cultural imperative facing artist and critic is the task of creating and approaching art in a manner which is both instrumental – 'modifying consciousness' – and therapeutic – opening up new forms of feeling and perception: 'What is important now is to recover our senses. We must learn to *see* more, to *hear* more, to *feel* more' (*AI* 14).

It is in the context of this concern with a widespread 'sensory anaesthesia' that Sontag makes her famous claim 'In place of a hermeneutics we need an erotics of art' (*AI* 14) – the statement which closes her 'Against Interpretation' manifesto. This privileging of the 'sensory experience' of art leads her to champion certain forms and mediums over others. Literature is clearly relegated as she finds it overly burdened with social and moral reportage, although she does value the 'new formalism' of French writing for its exploration of the formal textures of language and rejection of psychological profundity. In film, Happenings, and some forms of Pop Art she finds the sensual immediacy she is looking for, and favours film in particular for foregrounding 'the pure, untranslatable, sensuous immediacy' of the image – in the films of Bergman, Godard, and Resnais she relishes a 'liberating anti-symbolic quality' (*AI* 11). For all her levelling of cultural judgements and tastes Sontag has her own avant-gardist ideal, that of the uninterpretable text: 'Ideally, it is possible to elude the interpreters ... by making works of art whose surface is so unified and clean, whose momentum is so rapid, whose address is so direct that the work can be ... just what it is' (*AI* 11). While this remains an ideal it indicates that for Sontag art's greatest value resides in its *experience*, its processes and forms understood as modes of aesthetic apprehension. This prejudice towards the pheno-menological helps explain her interest in how formal innovations heighten perception and sensory awareness. Carrying such ideas into her reading of the new sensibility she applauds it for appealing not only to the intellect but to the body and locates in the sensual, libidinal energies of the new arts a challenge to the ascetic rational-ism of 'interpretation'.

Sontag's equating of sensuality with formalism is not a new idea – in the great thinkers of European aesthetics, Kant, Schiller, and Hegel we find the intellectual roots – and it is echoed in the contemporary cultural criticism of Herbert Marcuse and Norman O. Brown.[11] It is to traditions of aesthetic rather than hermeneutical thinking that she is drawn in so much of her work, most notably in *Against Interpretation* and *On Photography*. In these earlier essays she shows herself to be particularly interested in how the new arts expand or deconstruct 'the idea of art' and refer the reader, listener, or viewer to the nature of the art experience. Across several essays she explores what it means to have an aesthetic experience of the world and constructs an alternative genealogy of avant-gardism which draws together disparate aesthetic traditions and practices, European and American. It is in her concept of avant-gardism, in par-ticular, that Sontag's effort to critically map the new sensibility has its theoretical roots. By looking closely at this concept we shall also gain a fuller understanding of her considerable ambivalence about the 'culturally over-saturated' experience of American modernity.

Avant-garde and camp

Writing in 1957, Richard Chase began his essay 'The Fate of the Avant-Garde' by remarking that 'it is customary nowadays to pronounce the avant-garde dead'. He gives voice to the growing intellectual belief in the late 1950s that 'modernism and experimentalism in the arts is, after forty years of struggle, finally exhausted ... We now find ourselves in a period of suspended animation and cultural confusion.' But Chase remains optimistic that the 'recurring impulse to experimentation' and the 'polemical intransigence' of avant-gardism will reemerge in an active way in American culture. In the meantime, he argues, the 'avant-garde attitude' is kept alive in the 'flexibly dialectical mind of contemporary criticism'. For Chase, as for so many New York intellectuals of his generation, avant-gardism remains alive as an *idea* or attitude which critically refuses 'a formless middle way of feeling and thought'.[12] Sontag, too, is interested in the idea of the avant-garde as a cutting tool against social and intellectual complacencies, but she signals a new willingness to explore marginal and emergent 'sensibilities' and 'styles' which test the received wisdom that experimental aesthetics are absent from American culture and ask whether avant-gardism can regain any form of critical function at the very time it has become academicised and museum-bound.

Chase's refusal of 'a formless middle way of feeling and thought' is translated in the work of more hostile critics into a repudiation of all that is understood to be mass culture. As noted above, Clement Greenberg and Dwight Macdonald made sustained efforts to isolate and valorise avant-gardism in opposition to mass culture – a form of cultural boundary-drawing which took on a potent ideological significance in the anti-Stalinist context. Throughout the 1940s and 1950s Greenberg developed a very influential theory and critical history of the modernist avant-garde and we should note some of the key tenets of his theory here as they were certainly well known to Sontag.[13] Greenberg's argument in 'Avant-Garde and Kitsch' that the avant-garde promise to 'keep culture moving' is reformulated in specifically formalist terms in many later essays. At the heart of his neo-Kantian reading of modernism is the concept of artistic 'purity' predicated on a belief that the art object is self-contained and self-validating. Greenberg identifies and champions an aesthetic code in modernist art which acts as 'an ultimate, intrinsic value, an end-value, one that leads to nothing beyond itself'. He more particularly argues:

> It follows that a modernist work of art must try, in principle, to avoid communication with any order of experience not inherent in the most literally and essentially construed nature of its medium. Among other things, this means renouncing

illusion and explicit subject matter. The arts are to achieve concreteness, 'purity' by dealing solely with their respective selves – that is, by becoming 'abstract' or nonfigurative.[14]

For Greenberg, this 'non-representational' aesthetic is rigorously disciplined by a progressive history of formal innovation which he finds culminating in Abstract Expressionism in his own time. Further in line with this hermetic development he argues that this aesthetic prescribes 'specific areas of competence' which purge extra-aesthetic considerations – painting, sculpture and architecture are recognisably distinct and defined fields of 'art'.[15]

There is a good deal in *Against Interpretation* which echoes Greenberg's views. Compare Greenberg's statement: 'The avant-garde poet or artist ... [creates] something valid solely on its own terms', with Sontag's claim in 'Against Interpretation' '*Transparence* is the highest, most liberarating value in art – and in criticism – today. Transparence means experiencing the luminousness of the thing in itself, of things being what they are' (*AI* 13). Sontag shares something of Greenberg's high formalist pedigree, in particular an interest in the absolutist impulse in modernism to produce artworks which neither require nor demand extra-aesthetic 'justification' (*AI* 27). And like Greenberg she values the critical self-consciousness of modern art, what she calls its 'history mindedness', as an internal motor of formal evolution: 'The history of forms is dialectical ... forms in art are, periodically, exhausted. They become banal, unstimulating, and are replaced by new forms which are at the same time anti-forms' (*AI* 180). Moreover, Sontag is happy to underline the 'difficulty' of avant-garde art as a positive and necessary critical demand on its audience, as she recognises much of it is '*not* open to the generally educated; it demands a special effort ... and an education of sensibility' (*AI* 295).

However, while Sontag draws on these conventionalised views of avant-garde 'progress' she critically deploys them to support a new programme for experimentalism which is anathema to Greenberg. Before looking at how she does this we should note that a striking feature of her promotion of avant-gardism is the self-conscious manner in which she uses avant-garde rhetoric; there is certainly an imperiousness in Sontag's comments on experimental aesthetics but also a marked degree of artifice. In 'Nathalie Sarraute and the Novel' (1963) she contends that if Anglo-American criticism is to witness a 'coming-of-age of the novel' a rigorous and even opportunistic didactic commitment is required. This will entail a commitment to all sorts of questionable notions, like the idea of 'progress' in the arts and the defiantly aggressive ideology expressed in the metaphor of the avant-garde ... And it will make self-conscious aestheticians, didactic explorers, of all who wish seriously to practice the form ... the price must be paid. Readers must be made to see, by a new generation of critics who may well have to force this ungainly period of the novel down their throats by all sorts of seductive and partly fraudulent rhetoric, the necessity of this move. And the sooner the better. (*AI* 103)

This statement clearly foregrounds Sontag's own didactic ambitions in a manner which might be considered insulting to readers and critics if its aggression was not so deliberately exaggerated in staged hyperbole. The passage transmits her sense of how exhausted the language of artistic 'progress' really is and she seems barely able to use this language in good faith. There is a disingenuity in this passage (and there are many like examples in *Against Interpretation*) that works to provisionalise the arguments advanced. This is not to say, simply, that Sontag does not mean what she says – she is clearly drawn to demanding avant-garde aesthetics and privileges an austere formalism – but her arguments are often strategic, self-consciously positioned in relation to conventionalised cultural assumptions and seeking a new angle of perception on terms and ideas normalised with overuse.

In *Against Interpretation* Sontag seeks to reinvigorate the concept of the avant-garde by promoting it as a motor of aesthetic changes within an expanded field of art. In several essays she is fascinated with the new aesthetic relationships evident in multimedia 'spectacles' and in the hybridisations of form and genre which characterise the new sensibility. In her comments on new aesthetic formations such as Happenings, on the treatment of mass culture materials by artists, and on the camp sensibility she examines how avant-gardism has entered into a new relationship with the social conditions of mechanical reproduction and urban living. When she commends the work of John Cage, Robert Rauschenberg, Andy Warhol and William Burroughs for 'changing the ground rules which most of us employ to recognise a work of art' (*AI* 298), she advances her argument that form develops dialectically in the relationship between art and anti-art, but she also means this to legitimate a greater freedom for the artist in exploiting materials and methods, drawing 'for example, from industrial technology, from commercial processes and imagery, from purely private and subjective fantasies and dreams' (*AI* 296). This new eclecticism finds one of its potent cultural moments in the emergence of the Happening in New York in the late 1950s. In her essay 'Happenings: An Art of Radical Juxtaposition' (1962) Sontag briefly charts the history of this 'new, and still esoteric, genre of spectacle' which exhibits a 'fondness for incorporating ready-made materials of no artistic prestige, particularly the junk of urban civilization' (*AI* 269). Happenings are difficult to define in conventional art history terms, and Sontag clearly relishes this:

> The Happening takes place in what can best be called an 'environment', and this environment typically is messy and disorderly and crowded in the extreme, constructed of some materials which are rather fragile, such as paper and cloth, and others which are chosen for their abused, dirty, and dangerous condition. The Happenings thereby register (in a real, not simply an ideological way) a protest against the museum conception of art – the idea that the job of the artist is to make things to be preserved and cherished.   (*AI* 268)

On Sontag's reading, Happenings are frequently violent, always physical, their essence is tactility and immediacy; in their 'deliberate impermanence' and audience involvement they mock museum culture and the concomitant high culture values of seriousness and contemplation.

The Happening, in blurring the realms of 'art exhibit and theatrical performance' (*AI* 263), signalled a new experimentalism with intermedia art forms in the 1960s which developed rapidly throughout the decade. For Clement Greenberg and his followers such a blurring of artistic realms by Happenings and various forms of Pop and minimalist art transgressed the modernist code of aesthetic purity they championed. Michael Fried, a neo-Greenbergian academic, famously argued in the mid-1960s that 'art degenerates as it approaches the condition of theater', where 'theater' is 'what lies between the arts'.[16] For Sontag, 'what lies between the arts' are potentially new sites of aesthetic experimentation and negation and the clear implication in many of the *Against Interpretation* essays is that these new sites are in need of critical exploration if the avant-garde is to be a viable critical concept. Central to this critical project is her promotion of an alternative tradition of avant-gardism, based on Surrealism.

In her essay on Happenings Sontag offers a definition of Surrealism that goes well beyond the confines of 'a specific movement in painting' to describe

> a mode of sensibility which cuts across all the arts in the 20th century. There is a Surrealist tradition in the theater, in paint-ing, in poetry, in the cinema, in music, and in the novel ... The Surrealist tradition in all these arts is united by the idea of destroying conventional meanings, and creating new mean-ings or counter-meanings through radical juxtaposition ... Art so understood is obviously animated by aggression, aggression toward the presumed conventionality of its audi-ence and, above all, aggression toward the medium itself.
>
> (*AI* 269)

This view of Surrealism as a 'sensibility' which cuts across all the arts is crucial to Sontag's promotion of the new sensibility and her thoughts on modernity. It is a view which clearly informs several key arguments and propositions in *Against Interpretation*. Firstly, it allows her to construct an alternative genealogy of experimental modernism which is largely alien to the United States and which seeks to recuperate and conjoin the energies of what have been seen as isolated creative practices – one example is her linkage of Antonin Artaud's prescriptions for a 'theater of cruelty' to the violence of the Happening (*AI* 272-3). Secondly, her view that private fantasies are a legitimate and fecund subject for art and literature draws on the Surrealist insight that 'the meaning of modern art is its discovery beneath the logic of everyday life of the alogic of dreams' (*AI* 271). This insight is, as we shall see, a significant influence on her first novel *The Benefactor* and on her views on pornographic literature. Thirdly, she finds that Surrealism's 'witty appreciation of the der-elict, inane, *démodé* objects of modern civilization' (*AI* 271) is present in camp. Finally, and perhaps most importantly in the context of her stated concerns about the desensitising forces of modernity, she believes Surrealism offers art a social function which is both satirical and therapeutic. The satire rests in the 'dreamlike' mix of terror and comedy of Surrealism, which has its social correlative in the extent to which 'modern experience is char-acterized by meaningless mechanized situations of disrelation' (*AI* 274). Sontag also speculates that the Surrealist principle of radical juxtaposition can function in a progressive social and psychological manner, for she believes it can be conceived 'therapeutically – for the purposes of re-educating the senses (in art) or the character (in psychoanalysis)' (*AI* 271).

We can see how Sontag might be drawn to this therapeutic impulse as a possible counter to the 'sensory anaesthesia' she associates with the dominance of instrumental reason in her contemporary social world. In this, and in her positive assessments of Surrealism's satirical relationship to an urban environment of 'brutal disharmony' and mass culture 'detritus', she echoes some of the practitioners and fellow travellers of the Surrealist movement in the early twentieth century. When André Breton identified an 'explosion of dissent' among the avant-garde arts in the 1920s he signalled a new sense of attack on concepts of the organic unity and uniqueness of the work of art which separated it from social experience. For many Surrealists an interrogation of the autonomy of the aesthetic was necessary to expose the false separation of aesthetic and social realms. They saw social reality, especially that of modern urban life, as deeply encoded with aesthetic significance and their art works playfully juxtapose and deconstruct oppositions of image and reality, and surface and depth. As Walter Benjamin remarked of the Surrealists, 'life only seemed worth living where the threshold between waking and sleeping was worn away in everyone as by the steps of multitudinous images flooding back and forth, language only seemed itself where sound and image, image and sound interpenetrated with such felicity that no chink was left for the-penny-in-the-slot called "meaning"'.[17] Benjamin himself was drawn to Surrealism, finding in its juxtapositions of 'banal' everyday objects a 'profane illumination' of a new order of reality in the world of mechanical reproduction. As art lost its 'auratic' or cultic qualities he saw new possibilities for sensory experience and even radical poltical consciousness being opened up.[18]

Sontag shows little direct interest in new political possibilities but it is clear she adopts something of Benjamin's (partly forced, dialectically necessary) optimism about a nonauratic art affording new sensory stimulus. We can see that one of the central claims of *Against Interpretation*, that 'Art today is a new kind of instrument, an instrument for modifying consciousness and organizing new modes of sensibility', has theoretical foundations in her distinctive reading of Surrealism. For Sontag, Surrealism posits an intense yet playful commitment to the anti-artistic extremes of the central principle of modernism as a 'tradition against itself'. (For Clement Greenberg, notably, Surrealism was a threat to his tradition of avant-garde isolationism and he dismissed it as appealing merely to those 'repelled by the asceticisism of modern art'.)[19] At the same time, Sontag also extends the Surrealist interest in identifying new sites where diverse social and aesthetic forces interact. However, the positive charge she lends this interaction in her essay on Happenings dissolves elsewhere in *Against Interpretation* (and in her early fictional writings) into a more tentative sounding of, and ambivalent response towards, the social and moral implications of an aestheticisation of life. Walter Benjamin notes that an important social reason for the 'decay of aura' is the 'desire of contemporary masses to bring things "closer" spatially and humanly'.[20] Sontag is uneasy about this process, and in 'Notes on Camp' she provides a complex response to the synchronic present, one which indicates her truly ambivalent feelings about the 'culturally over-saturated medium in which contemporary sensibility is schooled' (*AI* 288).

In 'Notes on Camp' Sontag identifies camp as one of the three 'great creative sensibilities', the others being 'the seriousness … of high culture' and 'the extreme states of feeling' in avant-garde art (*AI* 287). Camp is 'the sensibility of failed seriousness, of the theatricalisation of experience'; it 'is the consistently aesthetic experience of the world' (*AI* 287). While distinguishing here between camp and the avant-garde 'seriousness whose trademark is anguish, cruelty, derangement', she does recognise that the wit and humour of Surrealism, and in particular its poeticisation of the banal, has a place in camp. She also points to its affiliations with homosexual culture, recognising that 'Camp taste' has acted as 'a gesture of self-legitimation' for homosexuals who have 'pinned their integration into modern society on promoting the aesthetic sense' (*AI* 290). Yet she believes that 'Camp taste is much more than homosexual taste' for it is 'part of the history of snob taste', signifying an 'aristocratic posture' which persists 'in increasingly arbitrary and ingenious ways' (*AI* 291). It is a taste 'possible only in affluent societies, in societies or circles capable of experiencing the psychopathology of affluence' (*AI* 289). It is on this point that Sontag touches most directly (given the deliberate shifts of argument and emphases effected by her fragmented 'Notes') on camp's contemporary social function. In the culturally saturated, affluent society camp offers a survival of style. Camp is not mass culture, rather it is an aesthetic lens through which to view mass culture, and a highly discriminating lens at that. And so:

> Camp is the answer to the problem: how to be a dandy in the age of mass culture. The connoisseur of Camp has found … ingenious pleasures … in the arts of the masses. Mere use

does not defile the objects of this pleasure, since he learns to possess them in a rare way. Camp ... makes no distinction between the unique object and the mass-produced object. Camp taste transcends the nausea of the replica.

(*AI* 288-9)

Camp can function as an ironic intellectual defence system; it offers the taking of pleasure in 'the arts of the masses' but also detachment from them by the imposition of a screen of taste.

It is not surprising that camp should hold a strong appeal for Sontag given its self-conscious artificiality and emphasis on 'texture, sensuous surface, and style at the expense of content' (*AI* 277). Although she is careful to note that camp is an amorphous and 'fugitive sensibility' it is clearly linked to the new sensibility. In the early 1960s a camp 'relishing' of mass culture is evident in the underground films of Kenneth Anger, Jack Smith, Andy Warhol, and Jonas Mekas, in the plays of Edward Albee, and in the poetry of Frank O'Hara and John Ashberry. In a short essay on Jack Smith's *Flaming Creatures* in *Against Interpretation* Sontag describes the film as a 'triumphant example of an aesthetic vision of the world' and remarks on how it creates a distinctively artificial environment of 'banal songs, ads, clothes, dances, and above all, the repertory of fantasy drawn from corny movies' (*AI* 230-1). Camp also appeals to Sontag in its inversion of values of 'moral seriousness' and 'judgement' to favour 'playfulness' and 'appreciation'. Part of the appeal may have been camp's irreverent response to critical values dear to many New York intellectuals. The essay certainly provoked negative responses from several New York critics, some of whom were astonished that *Partisan Review* could have published it.[21]

While there is much in camp that appeals to Sontag she could not be said to unequivocally champion it for her essay sounds a sharp note of ambivalence. Though she is vague about her reasons for such ambivalence it clearly owes something to the more general cultural conditions which give rise to camp as 'Dandyism in the age of mass culture' (*AI* 289). When 'modern experience ... [is] characterised by meaningless mechanised situations of disrelation' camp makes a virtue of this. The connoisseur of camp is a form of 'bricoleur', playing with self and experiences in a highly stylised manner without any ontological unease: 'To perceive Camp in objects and persons is to understand Being-as-playing-a-Role. It is the farthest extension, in sensibility, of the metaphor of life as theater' (*AI* 280). Camp offers an ironic response to the ephemerality of commercial culture and also to the metatheme of alienation that so characterised 1950s sociological and artistic expression. The anguished, nomadic self of the moderns is parodied if not simply rejected by camp. But camp in turn may be seen to promote a psychological inertia in its interfusion of reality and spectacle. Sontag states that camp is a 'feat goaded on, in the last analysis, by the threat of boredom' (*AI* 289). Perhaps, but a key implication of her essay is that it is grounded in a historical anxiety about the sense of self and that its passivity, detachment, and amorality signify a defensive retreat from social experience as much as a sophisticated manipulation and appropriation of mass culture objects and styles. This may explain why, in her preface to 'Notes on Camp', she states: 'I am strongly drawn to Camp, and almost as strongly offended by it' and refers to 'a deep sympathy modified by revulsion' (*AI* 276). Although she does not elaborate upon these comments I would argue that her understanding of camp as 'an experience of under-involvement, of detachment' (*AI* 291) posits so extreme a neutrality of feeling and so flattens the ethical landscape that she must express her ambivalence.

'Notes on Camp' offers a sophisticated response to a 'culturally over-saturated' American society. It moves well beyond the balkanisation of cultural 'levels' common to New York intellectual writing in the 1940s and 1950s, yet echoes something of that earlier critical unease about the cultural changes wrought by mass reproduction. With *Against Interpretation* Sontag ushers in a new artistic (and critical) pluralism and eclecticism, but not with the free abandon she was often accused of. Camp, she points out, proposes a democracy of taste in a manner which secures its own 'snobbery' of taste. In this it provides a figure for Sontag's own treatment of mass culture: she is prepared to celebrate it, but only when it is recuperated as art. Her approach is to be 'generous' (a phrase she uses approvingly on several occasions when describing the new sensibility challenge to high culture) and inclusive, bringing more various experiences into the province of aesthetic consideration. This is not to slight her real and provocative challenge to the hermetic 'idea of the modern' which is disdainful of 'the mass, the mire, the street'.[22] Sontag eschews such disdain for her aim is to reexamine and promote a new critical consciousness of the long-established, dialectical relationship between modernism and mass culture. This, for all the ambivalence and dubiety of her approach, is one of the important critical functions her early essays performed: identifying a significant advance in this dialectic in the early 1960s.

Art, eros, and morality

> The culture heroes of our liberal bourgeois civilization are anti-liberal and anti-bourgeois; they are writers who are repetitive, obsessive, and impolite, who impress by force – not simply by their tone of personal authority and by their intellectual ardor, but by the sense of acute personal and intellectual extremity. The bigots, the hysterics, the destroyers of the self – these are the writers who bear witness to the fearful polite time in which we live ... Ours is an age which consciously pursues health, and yet only believes in the reality of sickness. The truths we respect are those born of affliction.
>
> (*AI* 49)

These comments, from the beginning of a short essay on Simone Weil (1963), succinctly outline Sontag's sense of a central paradox of cultural modernism, that its iconoclastic writers and thinkers are valued less for their ideas than for the authenticity of their transgressions. 'For the modern consciousness', she remarks in another essay, 'the artist (replacing the saint) is the exemplary sufferer' (*AI* 42). Sontag shows herself to be a cold analyst of the romantic cult of suffering in modernist thought, and sceptical of the cultural democratisation of the private angst and anxiety of the moderns. 'Nihilism', she wryly observes, 'is our contemporary form of moral uplift' (*AI* 149). Yet, as we shall see, she has her own critical stake in what she terms 'the contemporary taste for the extreme in art and thought' (*AI* 50).

Sontag's modernist interest in forms of 'acute personal and intellectual extremity' in some part echoes but also departs from that of Lionel Trilling. Given his belief in the humanising role of culture Trilling always insisted on the social and moral bearing of consciousness. He repeatedly emphasised his distrust of any conception of art that proposed autonomy of self or form. A distrust of the powerful attractiveness of social disengagement in modernist writing is present in his famous thoughts 'On the Teaching of Modern Literature' (1966). He is wary, in this essay, of the modernist determination to explore the unconscious of the isolated self – often to cultivate what Thomas Mann called a 'sympathy for the abyss' – in attempts to locate or establish some form of 'other reality' or semi-conscious realm beyond that of contemporary social life. Modernist writing, he remarks, has the 'clear purpose of detaching the reader from the habits of thoughts and feeling that the larger culture imposes'; it seeks 'freedom from society itself'. The danger, for Trilling, is that this idea of 'freedom' compels commitment from students and teachers, commitment to socially and morally dubious ideas: 'the idea of losing oneself up to the point of self-destruction, or surrendering oneself to experience without regard to self-interest or conventional morality'.[23]

It is these very ideas of self-loss and surrender that attract Sontag to modernist writers and thinkers. In *Against Interpretation* she identifies a passionate and often perverse will to knowledge in the work of Weil, Sartre, Camus, Jean Genet, Cesare Pavese, and Michael Leiris. She is fascinated by the diminutions and recuperations of self-identity and understanding that characterise those modernists engaging 'the frustrations of consciousness, the dead ends of the self' (*AI* 42). What is at issue in this wilfulness is subjectivity. Of Sartre she notes: 'All relations ... are analysed as gestures of consciousness, appropriations of the other in the interminable self-definition of the self' (*AI* 98). She finds in Pavese's diaries a writer involved in a 'heroic quest for the cancellation of the self' (*AI* 43), while Leiris 'writes to appall ... haunted by a sense of the unreality of the world, and ultimately of himself' (*AI* 64). Extreme exacerbations of subjectivity and self-consciousness form a major theme in Sontag's writings. One of her earliest treatments of this theme is her first novel *The Benefactor* (1963).

The Benefactor may be read as an extended treatise on subjectivity; indeed it reads so much like a philosophical exercise that the characters merely seem vehicles for ideas. It deliberately eschews 'realistic' conventions of setting, character and plot – time and place are only very vaguely identified as prewar Paris. The novel, very self-consciously absurd in its pretensions, is an investigation of the possibility of a radical form of disburdenment, that of 'extinguishing' the self and erasing difference between self and world. Hippolyte, the protagonist, wants his dreams to direct his life: 'I [Hippolyte] was not looking for my dreams to interpret my life, but rather for my life to interpret my dreams' (*B* 41). His avowed desire is to achieve 'unity' through his dreams by allowing them to 'eradicate' thought (*B* 57). Seizing on 'the idea of being liberated through contradicting one's settled life and unleashing one's deepest fantasies' (B 74), he claims to live by the 'truth' of his dreams, and acts them out in an aesthetic and irrational existence. The idea of freedom announced here and which Hippolyte tries to attain – 'to escape having a personality' – is, he knows, morally and socially reprehensible judged by the norms of his society. Sexuality and crime appeal to him as attractive resources of the impersonal, but he finds for the purpose of the freedom he desires that 'there is something even more valuable than sexuality and crime ... There is the dream ... I am surprised dreams are not outlawed. What a promise the dream is! How delightful! How private! One need not enlist the cooperation of anyone, female or male (B 96-7).

The dream state challenges Hippolyte's powers and eventually his urge to interpret. Although he first responds to his dreams by attempting to interpret them he soon gives this up, asking: 'Why not take the dreams at face value?' (B 55). In order to do this, he believes

> A total attention was all that was required. In a state of total attention, there are no dark corners, no sensations or shapes that repel, nothing that seems soiled. In a state of total attention, there is no place for interpretation or self-justification or propaganda on behalf of the self and its resolutions.
>
> (B 145)

Hippolyte's dreams initiate a movement towards silence, as he learns 'from the dreams how to pursue them better. The dreams taught me the secret of perpetual presentness, and freed me from the desire to adorn my life and my conversation' (B 114). *The Benefactor* works to reflect the imaginary democracy of the dream state in which all phenomena – dreams, real events, and memory – are given equal significance, which is to say that there is no hierarchy of significance ordering or priming interpretation. We are told, for example, of Hippolyte's murder of his mistress Frau Anders that it came to seem to him 'more and more like a dream – all throbbing image, no consequences' (B 144).

For the reader, the text effects a similar reduction of significance and could even be said to impart something of a hallucinatory 'throbbing' of associations in that it deliberately undermines any clear narrative line as causal sequence. Repetition is a key motif in the dreams, and in the text. At one point Hippolyte appears to comment on this when he compares acting to dreaming: 'Those things we do well', he considers, 'are those we do over and over, and best are those which have themselves an essentially monotonous form: dancing, making love, playing a musical instrument' (B 103). These acts, which repeatedly appear in his dreams, are posited as acts without consequences; as with the dreams themselves they promise a zero degree of mediation or self-consciousness. Repetition also signifies equivalence and obsession, features of Hippolyte's narrative which he happily points to: 'That only one passion, or one idea, be made clear is task enough to fill a hundred volumes' (B 117). Absorbed in his dreams he believes that 'from monotony comes purity' (B 204); though this 'purity' seems less a death of consciousness than an absurd refinement of it (and narrative) as a machine of repetitions.

In both dreams and narrative, where reduction, contraction, and repetition are valued over adornment, expansion, and development, Hippolyte is learning 'disinterested surrender' (B 249). But he is frustrated by mediacy for all his attempts to surmount this problem, as language remains a stubborn interference to his idealised state of total attention. Wanting his dreams 'to be bare and taciturn' he finds instead that 'they were not laconic but full of conversations' (B 110). He announces an acute suspicion of language: 'I came to understand that words coerce the feelings they attempt to embody. Words are not the proper vehicle for a general upheaval which destroys the old accumulation of feeling' (B 63). This sense of language as an obstacle to the idealised state of total attention has significant psychoanalytic implications and indeed the novel shows the imprint, often ironically, of psychoanalytic theorising. Hippolyte's notion of 'total attention' is a figure for what in some forms of post-Freudian theory is recognised as an imaginary state of non-differentiation, a dyadic relation of wholeness between self and world. Language corrupts this ideal state; it signifies lack or loss and opens up the 'wound of subjectivity'.[24] The verbalisation of Hippolyte's loquacious dreams suggests that language defers the satisfaction of lost unity and that in this conflict of language and desire the unconscious is made manifest. His sense of ontological insecurity is emphasised within the text by the straining of boundaries between dream state and waking life. He hopes that these two realms will 'with perseverance and attentive inactivity … come together – even though it might be necessary to spend my life before a mirror' (B 187). Hippolyte and his reflections are never united though, much as they are confused for the reader, as the separateness of the image or the mediacy of language always reaffirms the sense of loss and dissolution imbricated in selfhood.

Sontag's elaborate exploration of the imaginary oscillations of identity is a highly ironic treatment of philosophical and psychoanalytic ideas, as the end of the novel underlines. Hippolyte, who refers to himself at the beginning of the text as the 'elderly scribe to my younger self' (B 12), is a somewhat duplicitous narrator. In the final chapters, as he muses on his life's accomplishments, he tells us that he has come across 'certain letters and journals which challenge my memory in its entirety. Perhaps it would be best for me to present some excerpts from these and leave the reader to decide for himself' (B 264). One notebook 'is in the third rather than the first person' and among the letters he finds is one briefly recounting his life story utilising details and fragments from his dreams as autobiographical fact. The metafictional stress on writing, reading, and interpretation serves to underscore the decentring of subjectivity the novel is so absorbed with at a thematic level, but it also foregrounds the agency of Hippolyte as a 'scribe' of his experiences. While offering no simple answers to the existential and ontological questions it very self-consciously raises, *The Benefactor* ultimately parodies the solipsism which erases the will to be in the world.

The Benefactor offers a complex allegory and some mockery of the modernist myth of a total self-sufficiency and privatisation of human experience. Hippolyte's experiment is 'to live out to the fullest the meaning of privacy' (B 95), an experiment evident in many of the novel's French intertexts, from Sade's *Justine* to Jean Genet's *The Thief's Journal*. In such texts extreme forms of negation strip characters of personality, obliterate will, and perversely identify 'freedom' in the absolute surrender of self to immediate (often violent) experience. Given the irony with which she treats these ideas we may say that Sontag is casting a sceptical critical eye on their implications when they are posited as foundations for a philosophy of life. Yet, if she treats these ideas with some irony this does not register a repudiation of them so much as a testing out of their insights and limitations, and this is very much in line with her preoccupations on the relationship between aestheticism and morality in *Against Interpretation*. In 'On Style' (1965), she writes:

> Of course, we never have a purely aesthetic response to works of art ... But neither would it be appropriate for us to make a moral response to something in a work of art in the same sense that we do to an act in real life. I would undoubtedly be indignant if someone I knew murdered his wife and got away with it (psychologically, legally), but I can hardly become indig-

nant, as many critics seem to be, when the hero of Norman Mailer's *An American Dream* murders his wife and goes unpunished. Divine, Darling, and the others in Genet's *Our Lady of the Flowers* are not real people whom we are being asked to decide whether to invite into our living rooms; they are figures in an imaginary landscape. The point may seem obvious, but the prevalence of genteel-moralistic judgements in contemporary literary (and film) criticism makes it worth repeating a number of times. (*AI* 23)

Sontag does repeat her point, or variations on it, on several occasions in *Against Interpretation* and we need to consider its implications for her theorising on aesthetic experiences.

Sontag's comments on Mailer and Genet make explicit her sense that there is a critical need to defend the autonomy of the aesthetic imagination. This is clear again in her short essay on Jack Smith's film *Flaming Creatures*, where she argues:

The space in which *Flaming Creatures* moves is not the space of moral ideas, which is where American critics have traditionally located art. What I am urging is that there is not only moral space, by whose laws *Flaming Creatures* would indeed come off badly; *there is also aesthetic space, the space of pleasure*. Here Smith's film moves and has its being.
(*AI* 231, emphasis added)

In her efforts to defend art which has 'its being' in this space Sontag revamps quite conventional concepts of aesthetic 'pleasure' and 'style' for the new sensibility arts. In 'On Style' she argues that while art is never historically or epistemologically innocent (though it may aspire to be so) the knowledge it imparts 'is an experience of the form or style of knowing something, rather than a knowledge of something (like a fact or a moral judgement) in itself' (*AI* 22). This is hardly an original proposition, for she is saying that art gives us a form of non-conceptual knowledge, an argument which has a long formalist pedigree from Kant to the New Critics and beyond, and would find agreement among many more of her contemporaries than she seems prepared to acknowledge.[25] There is nothing new in privileging form as a means of aesthetic apprehension which isolates and makes singular specific feelings and actions. What lends her views a distinctive contemporary relevance is her insistence that art provides a non-conceptual – more particularly, sensual – mode of experience which has a moral import.

Sontag's argument that aesthetic and moral responses to a work of art are not independent of one another rests on the (pheno-menological) premise that 'morality is a form of *acting* and not a particular repertoire of choices' (*AI* 24). So understood, morality in-heres in artistic efforts to make singular such qualities as 'contem-plativeness, grace, intelligence, expressiveness, energy, sensuous-ness' (*AI* 25). She clearly formulates this argument as a response to moralising judgements on art or literature, such as the work of Mailer or Genet widely received in the early 1960s.[26] She refers to 'the passion of an entire culture ... to protect and defend values traditionally conceived as lying "outside" art, namely truth and morality, but which remain in perpetual danger of being compro-mised by art' (*AI* 22). Her treatment of the 'art versus morality' division echoes the general emphasis in *Against Interpretation* on undermining conventionalised cultural and aesthetic categories of judgement and taste in order to expand not only what may be defined as 'art' but the concept of aesthetic comprehension as a significant mode of cultural understanding.

Sontag's argument for 'an approach which considers works of art as living, autonomous models of consciousness' (*AI* 27) under-pins her 'generous' aestheticism for she believes this principle legitimises a great variety of subjects for artistic treatment, includ-ing the use of fantasy, the exploration of ideas and of 'extreme states' of consciousness. In her advocacy of this critical approach, as with so much else in *Against Interpretation*, she seeks to draw attention to and challenge the strictures of the liberal imagination. Like Lionel Trilling she accords modernist art and literature a tremendous prestige as a semi-autonomous sphere of negation which can act as a corrective to the social organisation of imaginative life. However, the more iconoclastic areas of European modernism to which Sontag is drawn were treated with suspicion by those New Yorkers whose intellectual outlook was shaped by the postwar climate of anti-Stalinism and debates on totalitarianism. For Trilling the radical negativity of much modernist art and literature posits a self-sufficiency of consciousness and an independence of will which deny any 'accord with humanity'.[27] Sontag is impatient with the unifying authority of liberal humanism. In 'On Style' she empha-sises the agency of 'will' in aesthetic experience, and develops the suggestive Nietzschean association, for she is discussing a form of will to power, art as the imprint of volition and desire. 'A work of art', she comments, 'proposes a type of experience designed to manifest the quality of imperiousness' (*AI* 22). Scorning what she views as liberal hypocrisy about this quality she privileges the transfiguring power of art and ideas in the work of the modernist 'bigots, the hysterics, the destroyers of the self' (*AI* 49).

There is a strain of idealism, of muted utopian thinking, shadowing Sontag's new sensibility consciousness raising. It is evident in her 'against interpretation' rhetoric, as when she states: 'The aim of all commentary on art now should be to make works of art – *and, by analogy, our own experience* – more, rather than less, real to us' (*AI* 14; emphasis added). Her stand 'against interpretation' involves asking for a new 'immediacy' and 'openness' of understanding which would enlarge human capacities to think and act in the world. The freedom her writing seeks is a distended perturbation of thought and feeling and an imaginative transcendence of constraints – social, moral, and linguistic. As Richard Gilman astutely comments, 'there arises an aura of will or wilfulness' in Sontag's early writings,

> a wish that something be true, an unavowed prescriptive desire … beneath the clean-functioning, superbly armed processes of her thought exists a confused, importunate, scarcely acknowledged desire that culture, the culture she knows so much about, be other than it is in order for her to be other than she is.[28]

I think Gilman is right, and Sontag's critical activity is one means of working out this 'prescriptive desire'. (As we shall see, ideas of self-transcendence develop into a key theme in her writings.) For all that Sontag intimates about a need for radical cultural change these early writings are notably disengaged from political issues. Her intellectual processes are conditioned by modernist self-sufficiency and self-reflexiveness – hence her difficulties in articulating a *political* mode of will – leaving the reader to suspect a highly aesthetic voice often more in communion with itself than with the world. The polemics in *Against Interpretation* are leavened by a studied coolness in her treatment of iconoclastic art and ideas and a marked ambivalence about acting as an advocate or an exponent of the new. It is with characteristic seriousness that she remarks in her prefatory note to *Against Interpretation*, 'in the end, what I have been writing is not criticism at all, strictly speaking, but case studies for an aesthetic, a theory of my own sensibility' (*AI* viii).

For all her sense of critical ambivalence about her subject matter Sontag's early writings were widely received as engaged and even definitive guides to an emergent cultural radicalism. Her essays had a major intellectual and cultural impact in the mid-1960s beyond anything she could have either imagined or manipulated. That they did so owes a great deal to the dialectical charge of her writings as they worked across conventionalised boundaries tacitly separating literary and visual cultures, moral and aesthetic ideas, and intellectual and bodily pleasures. Reviewers of *Against Interpretation* were quick to identify her as an intellectual 'swinger', a barometer of all that was radically chic in New York intellectual culture. In a review entitled 'Swingtime', in the *New York Review of Books*, Robert Mazzocco found the volume to be a 'trend-swept chronicle of cultural disturbances'.[29] Others casually linked avant-gardism and gender: 'The lady swings', wrote Benjamin DeMott in the *New York Times Book Review*, 'She digs the Supremes and is savvy about Camp ... She likes her hair wild and her sentences intense.'[30] Such popular images became fortified even as the implications of Sontag's writings were contested. While some dismissed her as lacking in intellectual seriousness and programme others claimed her for their own arguments or movements. Writing in 1968 Richard Gilman pictured her as 'a representative advanced consciousness', an avant-gardist situated at the cutting edge of 'the new' and so 'able to discern what actually is coming to be born'.[31] For Gilman, and for many since, Sontag was the avatar of an emergent postmodern culture.

Sontag was keen to express resentment at her avant-gardist celebrity. 'Despite all my exhoratory tone', she wryly declaims in a prefatory note published in the paperback edition of *Against Interpretation*, 'I was not trying to lead anyone into the Promised Land except myself.'[32] There was limited sympathy for such special pleading among those most parochially interested in New York intellectual culture who quickly perceived the challenge she posed to the critical orthodoxy of her predecessors and their more devout followers. The sense of a challenge was heightened for those intellectuals uneasy about what they perceived as the crass democratisation of modernism's antinomian energies and the massification of the 'adversary culture' (once the special province of an independent elite). There is a note of betrayal in Irving Howe's complaint that Sontag 'employs the dialectical skills and accumulated knowledge of intellectual life in order to bless the new sensibility' and lends credence to 'an impulse to shake off the burdens and entanglements of modernism'.[33] In one sense, Howe could not have been more wrong. In *Against Interpretation* Sontag clearly states her view that it 'is mandatory for any responsible critic today' to develop 'an intelligent involvement with the problems and objectives of "modernism" in the arts' (*AI* 92). Far from throwing off her modernist heritage she sought (with some optimism and 'fraudulent rhetoric') to revitalise it by emphasising the aesthetic and ironic strains it had always held. And yet Howe was not simply wrong, for he recognised how the challenge Sontag posed to the seriousness and authority of his New York intellectual generation had been widely taken up. For Howe, as for so many of Sontag's 'culture-hungry interpreters', she was the very face of the *zeitgeist*.

A SENSE OF AN ENDING

In her writings of the later 1960s and early 1970s Sontag places under detailed scrutiny the concept of 'radical will' in modernist thinking (including her own). In 'Against Interpretation' she charged critics with 'an obligation to overthrow any means of defending or justifying art which becomes particularly obtuse or onerous or insensitive to contemporary needs and practice' (*AI* 4-5). In the essays collected in *Styles of Radical Will*, written between 1966 and 1968, she is less interested in being at the cutting edge of this injunction. In these lengthier, more reflective essays she asks what remains of the 'permanent spiritual revolution' of modernism, of its assumption that art can be used for ontological transcendence. With an admixture of sympathy and scepticism she interrogates the assumptions underlying the progressive avant-gardist movement in her own time towards 'the most excruciating inflections of consciousness' (*SRW* 33). In these essays she explores a range of aesthetic, epistemological, and political implications of this move-ment. In 'The Aesthetics of Silence', the volume's lead essay, and in a closely connected essay on the philosopher E. M. Cioran, she analyses the impact of self-consciousness on modern art and aes-thetics. In essays on pornographic literature and on Jean Luc Godard and Ingmar Bergman she extends these abstract reflections into analyses of specific artistic strategies of reflexivity, silence, and transgression. In the final section of the volume she includes the first detailed accounts of her political thinking, with 'Trip to Hanoi', the final essay, showing her confronting the limitations of her own historical (Western) consciousness in Vietnam.

Styles of Radical Will provides a clear continuity of focus on modernist ideas of (self-)transcendence, but deliberately moves these towards a personal and political moment to suggest that the author has worked them through to a new vantage point. In this chapter I follow this narrative of engagement and disburdenment, but also draw in other of Sontag's writings from this period – the novel *Death Kit* (1967) and several uncollected political writings – which I believe are relevant to the themes of *Styles of Radical Will* and the intellectual journey it signifies.

Silence

In *Styles of Radical Will* Sontag identifies an urge to terminality, a sense of an ending, in modernist thinking as it founders under the perceived 'burden' of 'secular historical consciousness' (*SRW* 74). Our knowledge and our actions are devalued by our over-consciousness, she observes:

> Ours is a time in which every intellectual or moral event is absorbed by a predatory embrace of consciousness: historicising. Any statement or act can be assessed as a necessary transient 'development' or, on a lower level, belittled as mere 'fashion.' The human mind possesses now, almost as second nature, a perspective on its own achievements that fatally undermines their value and their claim to truth.
>
> (*SRW* 74)

This is still a form of complaint with interpretation, of course, but the complaint is more abstractly pitched here, directed – with some metaphysical dramatics – at the 'predatory embrace of consciousness'. To think through self-consciousness, that is to think beyond it, seems an insurmountable problem: 'There is no outflanking the demon of historical consciousness by turning the corrosive historicising eye on it' (*SRW* 75). In engaging this issue as a pressing intellectual problem she shares with many of her French contemporaries what she describes as a 'sense of standing in the ruins of thought and on the verge of the ruins of history and of man himself' (*SRW* 75). The link with French thinkers, such as Georges Bataille, Michel Foucault, and Jacques Derrida, different though their responses are, is that they all see themselves operating on what Derrida calls 'the eve and aftermath of philosophy'.[1] *Styles of Radical Will* reflects this broadly modernist sense of endings and beginnings, though for Sontag it is the endings which are more definitively being established.

In her essay on E. M. Cioran, 'Thinking Against Oneself' (1967), Sontag notes that Hegel anticipated the twentieth-century crisis in aesthetic thinking in his analysis of a loss of sensory unity and exacerbation of historical consciousness as preconditions which would leave art with a future of ever-diminishing returns. Surveying art of the mid-twentieth century Cioran finds Hegel's prediction more than fulfilled. In *The Temptation to Exist* (1956) he argues that self-consciousness has overtaken the artist to the point where art is no longer a transcendental or instinctual site:

> Next to the contemporary 'maker' with his sufferings and his sterility, the creators of the past seem embarrassingly healthy: they were not made anemic by philosophy ... These days no one escapes this exacerbation of the intellect and its corresponding diminution of instinct. The monumental, the spontaneously grandiose is no longer ... The best thing an artist produces now are his ideas on what he might have done ... No age has been so self-conscious.[2]

For many twentieth-century theorists the Hegelian notion of a 'withering away' of art has proved a seemingly inevitable consequence of aesthetic thought. Theodor Adorno, for example, notes that: 'The revolt of art which programmatically defined itself in terms of a new stance towards the objective, historical world has become a revolt against art'; and, as he shrewdly puts it: 'Aesthetics today is powerless to avert its becoming a necrologue of art.'[3] The question aesthetics must pose to art is: 'What is art?' and the convulsive, incessant claims for the death of art ensue. Sontag is entering into this broad and complex debate. She could be said to have already participated in it in *Against Interpretation* as the question of what constitutes a work of art is ever-present in that volume. But it is present in the engaged sense of challenging and revising specific cultural and critical discourses and assumptions. In 'The Aesthetics of Silence' and 'Thinking Against Itself' she takes a step back, as it were, to investigate, at a more abstract level, broader aesthetic issues, though still with an eye on her contemporary cultural context.

In 'The Aesthetics of Silence' Sontag sets out to demystify the myth of 'the absoluteness of the artist's activity' (*SRW* 4): a myth which is a model of transcendence, aimed at 'the completion of human consciousness' (*SRW* 3). Viewing art as 'a particularly adaptable site on which to stage the formal dramas besetting consciousness' she argues that it has developed towards a crisis of reflexivity wherein it is no longer viewed as 'an expression of human consciousness' but rather as form of self-estrangement: 'Art is not consciousness *per se*, but rather its antidote – evolved from within consciousness itself' (*SRW* 4). This modernist turn implicitly rehearses an absolutist and paradoxical project, that of transcending mediation or, more apocalyptically, destroying art: if art is to aspire to 'an absolute state of being' it 'must tend toward anti-art, the elimination of the "subject" (the "object", the "image"), the substitution of chance for intention, and the pursuit of silence' (*SRW* 4-5). Silence, though, can only be a 'horizon' or 'boundary notion', always signifying the artist's clash with the inevitability of mediacy, that which cannot be overcome, transcended, or abolished:

> the very concreteness of the artist's tools (and, particularly in the case of language, their historicity) appears as a trap. Practised in a world furnished with second-hand perceptions, and specifically confounded by the treachery of words, the artist's activity is cursed with mediacy. Art becomes the enemy of the artist, for it denies him the realisation – the transcendence – he desires. (*SRW* 5)

As art both promises and denies transcendence, a 'new element enters the individual artwork and becomes constitutive of it: the appeal (tacit or overt) for its own abolition – and, ultimately, for the abolition of art itself' (*SRW* 4-5).

Silence can only exist figuratively; in artistic practices it is present as a rhetorical trope signifying 'the wish for a perceptual and cultural clean slate' (*SRW* 17). A distrust of language, Sontag observes, has promoted the use of silence as a significant trope in art that is 'privative', 'anemic', or 'impoverished' – she points to examples in the work of Gertrude Stein, Samuel Beckett, William Burroughs, John Cage, Ingmar Bergman, Jean Luc Godard, and certain Pop artists. With reference to these artists she proposes that: 'The art of our time is noisy with appeals for silence' – a paradox which encourages a highly self-reflexive response: 'One recognises the imperative of silence, but goes on speaking anyway. Discovering that one has nothing to say, one seeks a way to say *that*' (*SRW* 12). Sontag is somewhat sceptical of the minimalism, solipsism, and excruciating irony which can appear in art created with a consciousness of this paradox, and 'The Aesthetics of Silence' ends on a somewhat pessimistic note as she reflects on 'how far the resources of irony can be stretched' by self-consuming aesthetic projects. 'It seems unlikely', she concludes, 'that the possibilities of continually undermining one's assumptions can go on unfolding indefinitely into the future, without being eventually checked by despair or by a laugh that leaves one without any breath at all' (*SRW* 34).

While the main critical thrust of 'The Aesthetics of Silence' is her effort to demystify the myth of silence, there is clearly some ambivalence in Sontag's treatment of this myth. At times she sounds dismissive of its appeal, yet she also points to how it can produce vigorous artistic strategies and visions. While she never refers to her concept of an 'erotics of art' in these later essays it nonetheless shadows her arguments, as when she suggests that 'the notions of silence, emptiness and reduction sketch out new prescriptions for looking, hearing, etc. – which either promote a more immediate, sensuous experience of art or confront the artwork in a more conscious, conceptual way' (*SRW* 13). What fascinates her about the will to silence is its projected horizon, 'an anticipated radical transvaluation of human values' (*SRW* 18), and this remains compelling for her despite the compromised and increasingly attenuated claims of modernism as a secular religion. In her essays on Bergman and Godard, and more controversially in her essay on 'the pornographic imagination', she more fully explores the 'radical will' to confront and counter the constraints of intellectuality.

For Sontag, to at once recognise the imperative of silence yet go on speaking is to respond not merely to a formalist imperative to 'make it new' (or flee interpretation) but to an ontological imperative to struggle endlessly with negations and affirmations of consciousness. This aporia can lend silence an unnerving power, and this is precisely the subject of her essay 'Bergman's *Persona*' (1967). The film *Persona* concentrates on the relationship between an actress, Elizabeth, who is silent throughout most of the film and her nurse, Alma, who becomes increasingly distressed with this silence and obsessed by a need to make the actress speak. The facticity and opacity of this mute condition is at once that of the actress and of the film itself; the film enacts a 'calculated frustration of the desire to know', with the result that 'the audience is ... haunted ... by the sense of a lost or absent meaning' (*SRW* 133-4). If *Persona* has a subject, Sontag proposes, it is 'the depths in which consciousness drowns', 'the horror of the dissolution of personality' (*SRW* 142). The dissolution occurs in the power struggle between speech and silence. In this, language as speech comes to represent a violence, a violating attack on the other, but it is silence which dominates the relationship as it does the narrative. The nurse's composure disintegrates; the result is a collapse of language and self-identity which Sontag posits as 'the most powerful instance of the motif of exchange. The actress creates a void by her silence. The nurse, by speaking, falls into it – depleting herself' (*SRW* 144).

The relation between the actress and her nurse as Sontag presents it is analogous to that between artwork and interpreter. 'Against Interpretation' concerns are clearly present in the emphasis on the impossibility of hermeneutic closure: the actress/artwork refuses imputations of significance. What is more pronounced here in Sontag's writing on the uninterpretable is her concern with how 'opaqueness induces spiritual vertigo' (*SRW* 17). The silent artwork provides a number of symbolic functions as a screen onto which meaning and desire are projected only to be found lacking, insupportable. What she is exploring here is not the ineffability of art but the question of how an artwork may posit a kind of ontological defamiliarisation (a form of subliminal terror and exhilaration) by suggesting that the hermeneutical collapse of interpretation unsettles the illusory security of a self-sufficient ego. What is exposed, in other words, in the fitful glimpse of the radically other is the necessary reliance of the rational on the irrational, the self on the not-self, language on silence.

This nexus of relations is again foregrounded in the essay 'The Pornographic Imagination' (1967). At one level, this essay is a response to contemporary public arguments gathered around the issue of pornography, while at another (and more compellingly for its author) it is an inquiry into the relationship between desire and knowledge at 'the frontiers of consciousness' (*SRW* 45). The essay advances and expands upon concerns already present in *Against Interpretation*. In a short review of Norman O. Brown's *Life Against Death* Sontag had chastised 'contemporary American intellectuals' for not being 'serious or honest enough about sexuality', and pointed for contrast to a French intellectual tradition of discussion about 'the twin subjects of eroticism and liberty' (*AI* 257). It is to this tradition she looks in expounding her views on the pornographic imagination. Drawing on a tradition of French writing, from Sade to Georges Bataille, which has dealt with sexuality in terms of a 'loss of the self', she proposes that

> the obscene is a primal notion of human consciousness, something much more profound than the backwash of a sick society's aversion to the body ... Tamed as it may be, sexuality remains one of the demonic forces in human consciousness – pushing us at intervals close to taboo and dangerous desires,

which range from the impulse to commit sudden arbitrary violence upon another person to the voluptuous yearning for the extinction of one's consciousness, for death itself ... These phenomena form part of the genuine spectrum of sexuality, and if they are not to be written off as mere neurotic aberrations, the picture looks different from the one promoted by enlightened public opinion, and less simple.   (*SRW* 57)

This is one of the most striking points Sontag makes in her essay, underlining the significance of death and self-extinction in erotic obsession, and using this as a critical lever on conventionalised cultural definitions of 'sexuality'.

Sontag views the pornographic imagination as a 'post-religious' form of thinking, motivated by the possibility of self-transcendence. Of Pauline Reage's *Story of O*, she writes

O is an adept; whatever the cost in pain and fear, she is grateful for the opportunity to be initiated into a mystery. That mystery is the loss of the self. O learns, she suffers, she changes. Step by step she becomes more what she is, a process identical with the emptying out of herself. In the vision of the world presented by *The Story of O*, the highest good is the transcendence of personality. The plot's movement ... [is] a kind of ascent through degradation. O does not simply become identical with her sexual availability, but wants to reach the perfection of becoming an object.   (*SRW* 55)

Similarly, Sontag identifies an urge to transcendence in Bataille's concept of 'transgression' when she notes that he views 'the extremity of erotic experience' as 'the root of vital energies. Human beings, he says ... live only through excess. And pleasure depends on "perspective", or giving oneself to a state of "open being," open to death as well as to joy' (*SRW* 61). It is excess, for Bataille, that disturbs the prohibitions of 'utilitarian' reason. Eroticism is viewed as a scandal to the economy of reason for 'erotic conduct is the opposite of normal conduct, as spending is the opposite of getting ... Pleasure is so close to ruinous waste that we refer to the moment of climax as a "little death".'[4]

On Sontag's reading, eroticism is excessive of structurally understood sexual relations. At the end of her essay she posits erotic transgression as a dialectical force which may take on a progressive function in a world of power–knowledge relations. She condemns

the traumatic failure of capitalist society to provide authentic outlets for the perennial human flair for high-temperature visionary obsessions, to satisfy the appetite for exalted self-transcending modes of concentration and seriousness. The need of human beings to transcend 'the personal' is no less profound than the need to be a person, an individual. But this society serves that need poorly. It provides mainly demonic vocabularies in which to situate that need and from which to initiate action and construct rites of behaviour.   (SRW 70)

The pornographic imagination, she suggests, has 'its peculiar access to some truth ... about sensibility, about sex, about individual personality, about despair, about limits' (SRW 70-1), and so moves us towards knowledge that is not socially circumscribed: 'That discourse one might call the poetry of transgression is also knowledge' (SRW 71).

'The Pornographic Imagination' lends a socio-political context to the myth of transcendence inherent in the trope of silence. However, Sontag's efforts to employ the pornographic imagination in a negative dialectic (centred on a 'concern about the uses of knowledge itself' (SRW 71) in a capitalist society) are limited by her aesthetic interpretation of this imagination. She is notably selective in her analysis of 'pornographic literature' – French avant-garde writers – and while this may add to the polemic charge of the essay it also serves to bracket off many of the socio-moral questions central to the pornography debate and lends a haze of abstraction to her enterprise. (D. H. Lawrence would probably view her ideas on erotics as the ultimate sin of cerebral sex: 'sex-in-the-head'.) Although she believes that erotic transgression must finally be a socio-political issue she does little to situate the literature she examines, or ideas she picks up, historically. Nor does she specify the politics of desire as a social experience. Fredric Jameson has suggested that

> the right to a specific pleasure, to a specific enjoyment of the potentialities of the material body – if it is not to remain only that, if it is to become genuinely political, if it is to evade the complacencies of 'hedonism' – must always in one way or another also be able to stand as a figure for the transformation of social relations as a whole.[5]

I do not quote Jameson to imply that Sontag should have adopted a Marxist dialectics, but rather to suggest that although she seems to want to signify potential 'transformation of social relations' her '[legitimation] of a repressed faculty' does not successfully 'stand as a figure' for such a transformation.[6] (She neglects, moreover, to question the politics of the pornographic imagination in the sense that it could be said to take on deeply authoritarian implications. This is an issue – the interrelations of aesthetic and political wills to power – which I examine later as it is important to her thesis on fascist aesthetics.)

The essays in *Styles of Radical Will*, as we have seen, are closely focused on ideas of transcendence and transgression. Whether examining the silent artwork, or 'the horror of the dissolution of personality' in *Persona*, or 'Cioran's subject: on being a *mind*, a consciousness tuned to the highest pitch of refinement', or O's 'emptying out of herself', a rhetoric of loss and release predominates. These essays codify and add substantial textual detail to more fragmented comments in *Against Interpretation* on forms of 'acute personal and intellectual extremity'. The myth of silence holds some appeal for Sontag, committed as she is to 'the idea that the power of art is located in its power to *negate*' (*SRW* 8). With these essays she is feeling her way towards her own style of radical will, and each essay adds to this work-in-progress. The denouement of this particular intellectual and textual journey is 'Trip to Hanoi', wherein she confronts the vulnerability of her intellectual identity and tests her aesthetic will against political realities. Before turning to this essay and other of her political writings we shall look at how silence functions as a significant trope in her second novel *Death Kit*.

Death and the novel

Death Kit describes an extraordinary exacerbation of consciousness, the effort of its protagonist Diddy to journey 'into himself, away from all coherent rational spaces' (*DK* 105). This journey is recorded as a hallucinatory dream which he experiences as he lies dying on a hospital bed. Diddy is an educated copywriter for a New York optics firm who has given way to his 'ingenious sense of incapacity' (*DK* 14) and swallowed a bottle of sleeping pills. Although his attempt at suicide is successful Sontag withholds this information from us until the end of the novel, making of the preceding action a symbolic effort by Diddy to come to terms with his death by imaginatively constructing his own 'death kit', drawing up an 'inventory' of his life. We are again dealing with a drama of consciousness where, as Sontag says of E. M. Cioran's writings, 'thinking ... devours itself –

and continues intact and even flourishes, in spite (or because) of ... repeated acts of self-cannibalisation' (*SRW* 80). Diddy's 'mental disembowelment' recalls the efforts of Hippolyte in *The Benefactor* to extinguish personality, but this later novel (while also self-consciously plundering modernist ideas and styles) is more ambitious and compelling in its treatment of the prison-house of consciousness, lending this theme a pathos and, albeit obliquely, a contemporary social dimension missing from the earlier text.

Diddy's cultivation of interiority in some part reflects Sontag's admiration for modernist dramas of the desiccated or 'withdrawn consciousness' (*SRW* 17). He feels he is merely 'the tenant of his life' (*DK* 4) and experiences a hypersensitivity toward the physical world.

> Diddy, not really alive, had a life. Hardly the same. Some people are their lives. Others, like Diddy, merely inhabit their lives. Like insecure tenants, never knowing exactly the extent of their property or when the lease will expire. Like unskilled cartographers, drawing and redrawing erroneous maps of an exotic continent.
>
> Eventually for such a person, everything is bound to run down. The walls sag. Empty spaces bulge between objects. The surfaces of objects sweat, thin out, buckle. The hysterical fluids of fear deposited at the core of objects ooze out along the seams. Destroying things and navigating through space become laborious. (*DK* 2)

Diddy's problem is not new, having existential credentials, echoing Sartre's *La Nausée* where 'everything that is exists in an opaque, meaningless thereness which spreads obfuscation and causes disgust', where the authentic 'privacy of the self' is assaulted by the public realm.[7] Like Sartre's Roquentin, Diddy experiences nausea when confronted by the brute facticity of things, feeling thoroughly abstracted from a world beyond his control. Highly reflective rather than an initiator of action, he is an 'unskilled cartographer' (*DK* 78) who attempts to map out the contours of his life. The inference here is one of life lived at an intellectual remove and indeed the deadpan narrating voice does transmit something of that detachment laced with anxiety which Sontag associates with the trope of silence.

In describing an average day at Diddy's place of work Sontag apes the nouveau roman's focus on surface detail and works into this a sense of repressed horror at the formlessness of everyday experience:

Arrival at the office. His jellied porous boss, Michael C. Duva, advances across the floor with a file of correspondence between Watkins and Company and *The Review of Scientific Instruments* that needs Diddy's attention. Why does Duva tilt his head to the left when he speaks, why does he smile, and why does he allow those drops of saliva to collect at the corners of his mouth? Riding out the tide of nausea, Diddy fingers the scuffed aluminium of his desk and stares urgently at the water cooler. His cardboard secretary is at her post, surreptitiously adjusting her stockings. Diddy doesn't mind handling papers. But, immaculate always, he dislikes changing a typewriter ribbon. Is frustrated to the point of tears while making a sketch for a new layout, when a narrow line drawn with India ink arbitrarily thickens or swells into a stain.   (DK 8)

As in much of the narrative, time is compressed here into a continuous present, lending the text a peculiar effect of immediacy. The flatness of descriptive detail and emotional content is suggestive of an all inclusive (enclosing) present pressing on the perceiving consciousness. This only further concentrates our attention on the movements of Diddy's mind so that the seemingly inconsequential takes on the horror of the arbitrary, whether in Duva's movements or the staining of the ink. Sontag's anaemic descriptions of surface and detail focus the reader's attention on the kinetics of her protagonist's interior dilemma; in Diddy's sense of helpless detachment from purpose or meaning we feel we have access to a mind neurotically and obsessively turned in upon itself.

While this existential horror story clearly has its roots in European literature and philosophy it also has an American dimension. The idea of 'everything running down', of linguistic, cultural, and informational entropy, is a common motif in American literature of the 1960s. As Tony Tanner has observed: 'In the most general terms entropy is concerned with the fate of energy – the individual's, society's, the world's – and as such is well calculated to interest the novelist trying to discern what patterns the released powers and vitalities of his age and society are establishing.'[8] In *Death Kit* Diddy's America is a 'doomed place' where conscious space is rapidly being eroded away:

A railroad station is public space, open to anybody ... But as on every trip upstate to the plant in recent years, Diddy can't help remarking the steady deterioration of the surfaces and furniture of this station. On each arrival the floor, walls, columns, bronze statue, information booth, clock, ticket windows, newspaper stand, wooden benches look more indelibly stained and grimier and more thickly littered. Not only mere negligence is at work here, surely. A question of policy or principle. Only a matter of time before the wrecker's ball gets around to undoing this generous space, so that something smaller can be put up in its stead. But isn't there a good deal to be said for keeping a doomed place clean and in decent repair? The claims of dignity, for instance. Especially since nemesis is proving to be somewhat dilatory in paying its anticipated call.

(DK 44)

The process of 'steady deterioration' marks both public and private spheres in the novel. Communication breaks down as 'human speech ... declines into mere sound' (DK 4); watching television news broadcasts Diddy finds no 'information' being transmitted, merely lists of atrocities and trivialities delivered in a 'denatured voice' (DK 165).

One result of Diddy's retreat 'into himself, away from all coherent rational spaces', is that the public, socio-political world is all but exiled from his withdrawn consciousness. Yet Sontag has this world constantly intrude on his self-reflections, most significantly in several news reports on the Vietnam War. One report offers

Just more about the unspeakable war, the one in which territory doesn't change hands and the sole measure of each victory is how many small-boned yellow bodies, with flesh charred by napalm or shattered by metal, huddle and sprawl on the ground after the battle. Waiting to be counted. The newscaster deploys the usual senseless numbers; repeats the well-worn gruesome tautologies of self-righteousness. With a broadly serious set to his face. Lies, but terrible smiling lies.

(DK 165)

The war is literally 'unspeakable' in the novel – 'Vietnam' is never mentioned – and Sontag is clearly suggesting that the horror of the war numbs human responses and renders language incapable of expressing the reality (yet another meaning of 'silence'). The Vietnam War hovers in the background of the novel and there is no simple sense in which *Death Kit* is 'about' the war. But there is an allegorical edge to Diddy's journey towards death which implicates national as well as private questions of guilt and innocence. As he is 'reminded of the behaviour of his own country, currently engaged in the cumbersome, drawn-out murder of a small defenseless nation' Diddy wonders if the 'overkilling' (DK 167) in Vietnam threatens to diminish individual claims to guilt or innocence and to hollow out the meaning of individual acts of violence.

The meaning of Diddy's journey towards death is not reducible to a national allegory though, for Sontag has other meanings, psychological and reflexive, to explore. The novel is very self-consciously concerned with relationships between beginnings and endings: 'Knowing one has a life induces the temptation to give it up. One is dead. Therefore, one wants to die. Equally, one wants to be born.' (DK 6) The motor of this temptation is desire, which (as Sontag argues in 'The Pornographic Imagination') is always oriented towards death. Desire has a narrative impulse, a compulsion towards death, but it undergoes repetitions and detours in this movement, constantly approaching yet deferring its ultimate object. In the dreamscape of the novel desire is uncensored; as the antithesis of the rational self it shadows and subverts Diddy's efforts to imagine an order of things (an 'inventory') which would make his life meaningful. Diddy begins 'to doubt his memory' as all 'past events, both real and imaginary are consigned to the trusteeship of the imagination' (DK 35). In place of coherence and unity he must contend with dissolution and disconnection. His efforts to provide through memory and imagination an inventory of his life constitute a failure of conceptual synthesis. He is given to 'mixing up different domains of blindness and enclosure', and his reflections on his life are constantly tried by the 'subtle menace of uncertainty' (DK 124).

In Diddy's dream-narrative there are two significantly traumatic events – really the same event, repeated – the murder(s) of a workman by Diddy in a dark railway tunnel (one of many Freudian allusions in the text). The murder(s) lend Diddy's 'anxiety the form of enigma' (DK 145) – did he or did he not commit murder? – but the enigma is an illusion, a projected paradigm to enclose and order the arbitrary, alleviate anxiety, and raise the hope of resolution in conclusion. Nonetheless, the murder(s) have suggestive symbolic functions. They may signify Diddy's effort to project his suicide outwards; during the first act of murder he struggles with feelings that must have been bound up with his suicide: 'fake toughness', 'you asked for it, you bastard!', and 'Diddy considers the time before he struck the workman: his whole life' (DK 23-4). Diddy is now on 'the far side of the appalling moment' (suicide/murder) and 'looking back with anguished longing at the years behind, receding. Done, like a slice. Never to be undone' (DK 24). The act of murder also signifies that Diddy has taken on some vital (unconscious) energy, he is now a 'posthumous person ... [with] new resources' (*DK* 7) which will allow him to explore the 'far side' of death, that is the imaginary landscape of desire freed from conventional regulations. Following the second murder he calmly walks deeper into the tunnel 'looking for his death' (*DK* 291).

Only at this point, at the end of the narrative as he emerges from the tunnel into an equally darkened 'charnel house' consisting of a series of rooms each filled with images of death, does Diddy finally consider that 'perhaps he has the answer to that desperate thought about the world. Life = the world. Death = being completely inside one's own head' (*DK* 310-11). Significantly, at this point, he feels fully freed from the conventional concepts upon which he has had to judge his life – in particular, freed from questions of guilt (about his suicide/act(s) of murder). He finally feels 'absolved from the duty of classifying himself or appraising his surroundings' for he is with the dead for whom 'nothing could be less relevant ... than judgement. That's what death is about. They're all collected here, the guilty and the innocent, those who tried and those who didn't' (*DK* 310). The old dualities of guilt and innocence are irrelevant to Diddy in the space (of thought) he has entered, towards which his mind has inexorably if non-systematically 'tunnelled'. There is no neat closure to the 'enigma' of the murder, rather hierarchies and structures of value and judgement are flattened out as desire finds its ultimate fulfilment.

The ending of the novel returns us to the relationship between beginnings and endings and suggests a key to its reflexive aims. 'Death', Walter Benjamin famously observed, 'is the sanction of everything that the storyteller can tell.'[9] Benjamin links the human desire for knowledge of death to the imaginary closure of narrative which promises to confer meaning on the movement from beginning to end. As Peter Brooks, extending Benjamin's insight, puts it: 'All narrative may be in essence obituary in that ... the retrospective knowledge that it seeks, the knowledge that comes after, stands on the far side of the end, in human terms on the far side of death.'[10] The paradox of narrative is that it is simultaneously prospective and retrospective, it seeks a return to the end which is always already its moment of beginning. *Death Kit* both explicitly thematises this paradox and reflexively plays with it. The novel begins at the end, with Diddy's death, and makes of his dream a lengthy narrative postponement of (what has already been fulfilled) the 'temptation' to give up life. The 'enigma' of the murder is, on this reading, a plot device which offers to structure textual energies (Diddy's 'new resources') so as to underline the arbitrariness and illusionary nature of such structures and in particular of narrative closure. The enigma of death is also one of origins, and so, in the house of death, Diddy

> swarms with the happiness of being in his body, and feels his nakedness as a delicious blessing. His alert head; the strength of his supple feet traversing the cool stone flooring; the easy hang of his shoulders and the bunched muscles of his calves; his sensitive capacious chest; the hard wall of his lean belly; the tender sex brushing the top of his thighs. Astonishing, isn't it, that any infant human being ever surrenders such pleasures. (DK 311)

At the end of the novel Diddy returns to such pleasures, and dies.

What are we to make of this intensely reflexive treatment of psychological and narratological endings and beginnings? If we focus primarily on the narrative play then Sontag would appear to be pushing the 'aesthetics of silence' to the absurd limits she refers to in her essay, where she notes that irony threatens to displace any need to take seriously art's dealings with 'the most excruciating inflections of consciousness' (SRW 33). Is irony the key mode of narrative inquiry in *Death Kit*? It is certainly present, not least in Diddy's self-reflections, and indeed he is described as 'endowed with vast amounts of irony applied at his own expense' (DK 7). I believe Sontag, as author of the narrative, is also endowed with a considerable degree of irony, at the reader's expense. Throughout the novel Diddy's consciousness figuratively contracts within ever smaller 'spaces' and the novel might be read as a huge conceit or self-parody as the ending in particular implies, with Diddy seemingly disappearing into the tunnel of his consciousness in an extended and ludicrously exaggerated metaphor of self-erasure. In her essay, we recall, Sontag expresses some doubts about the resourcefulness and future of the aesthetics of silence: 'It seems unlikely', she concludes, 'that the possibilities of continually undermining one's assumptions can go on unfolding indefinitely into the future, without being eventually checked by despair or by a laugh that leaves one without any breath at all' (SRW 34). *Death Kit* may well be making its own commentary on such strategies as tantamount to a death kit for the novel as a genre.

However, I am reluctant to conclude with such observations for I believe that although irony undercuts the seriousness of Sontag's concerns in *Death Kit* it neither simply abolishes this seriousness nor invalidates the concerns. In *Death Kit* she explores the modernist cult of self-negation to reveal its absurdities and paradoxes. In his morbid self-absorption Diddy is the figure of the modernist writer who pushes the self to a state of crisis, yet his very horror at this crisis is also a form of pride in his highly refined intellectuality. The writer becomes wholly reliant upon the imagination in the hubristic act of constructing an 'inventory' of the world. Sontag is wary of this hubris, she cannot help but parody it, yet she also wants to affirm the autonomy of imaginative licentiousness and extremism. She keeps her distance from Diddy, reluctant to present him as an anti-hero, yet she also implies that his necromantic dream perversely dramatises the sense of an ending in late modernist culture.[11]

Political tourism

In her earliest writings Sontag avoids overtly political subject matter. In her first major political essay 'Trip to Hanoi' (1968) she describes herself as 'a stubbornly unspecialized writer who has so far been largely unable to incorporate into either novels or essays my evolving radical political convictions and sense of moral dilemma at being a citizen of the American empire' (*SRW* 205). The evidence of *Against Interpretation*, *The Benefactor* and *Death Kit* would seem to support this statement. However, prior to the writing of 'Trip to Hanoi' Sontag does give voice to her 'evolving' political views in several speeches, statements, and interviews in the mid-1960s. In a 1966 speech on 'The Role of the Writer as Critic' she expresses her belief in and commitment to the need for critical dissent:

> The role of the writer as critic or dissenter provides the key to everything serious that has happened in our culture in the last 100 years. The writer is the model of the awake consciousness. There are moments when the writer *must* step forward and speak out ... It is the natural extension of being who he is, seriously. And what his being political means, beyond his ordinary duties as a citizen, is his being a critic, frankly and unashamedly ... Right now, it seems to me one task of the American writer is to be yelling at the top of his voice at the folly and ugly self-righteousness, at the immorality of and terrible danger entailed by our government's policy and

behaviour in Vietnam ... Writers should be in the vanguard of the dissenting minority, those who have the courage to be afraid, those who say 'No', those who cry 'Stop.'[12]

Sontag signals here her identification with a conventionalised idea of the writer's role as dissenting critic, the 'awake consciousness' who imagines and speaks for a larger social or moral good – an ethic of dissent central to the critical identity of the New York intellectuals. In a 1968 interview she expresses her disgust with American foreign policy and comments: 'I guess what keeps me here is a sense of responsibility. I have no illusions about my power, but even if I affect only a handful of people, I feel obliged to stay here and speak.'[13]

An important element of Sontag's 'public intellectual' profile draws on her political position-taking from the mid-1960s onwards. Her political thinking has evolved markedly and has proved every bit as controversial as her aesthetic vanguardism. While her political comments are often passionate they also reveal a highly selective involvement in specific issues and heightened self-consciousness about taking on the dissenting voice. In the 1960s and early 1970s she regularly states her sympathies with both feminist and anti-war movements but never gives herself wholly to these or any other programmes for political and social change. What characterises her political essays and speeches is an effort to synthesise intellectual (self-)interest and political struggle, a sometimes precarious exercise which has frequently drawn strong criticism but which seems to be necessary to her if she is to write about political issues at all. When general political commentary is sought from her she can sound awkwardly polemical or uninformed. In 'What's Happening in America' (1966), her responses to a *Partisan Review* questionnaire on America's social ills and foreign policy, she offers mostly stale views on American violence and 'national psychosis', and hits a low point with her opinion that 'The white race *is* the cancer of human history' (*SRW* 203) – a remark she would later regret. What eludes her in these responses is a sure grasp of her subject and a formal means of convincingly expressing the grounds of her sense of political and moral outrage. 'Trip to Hanoi', in sharp contrast to such statements, offers a detailed meditation on her 'radical' values and assumptions.

First published in *Esquire* in 1968, 'Trip to Hanoi' records Sontag's thoughts on her visit to North Vietnam in May of that year as a 'guest' of the North Vietnamese government. While her experience in Vietnam clearly facilitates her expression of political and national concerns the essay is also continuous with her aesthetic theorising in this period. It is fitting that it should appear as the final essay in *Styles of Radical Will* where it serves to review and partially revise major themes of this volume by bringing into question the very grounds of Sontag's intellectual selfhood in national, cultural, and political terms. In 'Trip to Hanoi' she explores what is significantly Western and American about her own self-consciousness, considering the limitations of her own culturally formed modes of understanding and self-conception when confronted with Vietnam and its people. When the essay first appeared, though, there was limited critical sympathy for Sontag's treatment of her personal dilemmas. Reviewing the essay in the *New York Review of Books* Frances Fitzgerald applauded Sontag for foregrounding issues of interpretation and emphasising that 'the subject of the war has not been Vietnam itself, but the American perception of it'.[14] But the more general response on the liberal left was one of outrage and betrayal. As Lawrence M. Bensky recalls:

> inmates in the liberal and radical wards in the cultural asylum roared in pain. How dare Susan Sontag use the Vietnamese as foils for her own personal psychological development? How dare she claim to be a radical and still spend time agonising over agonising at the typewriter? Aren't we being gassed, clubbed, taxed, drafted, jailed while she is trying to decide what to say?[15]

The tone of the outcry suggested that she had failed to keep faith with the nature and atmosphere of 1960s radicalism in America, that this was not a time for self-questioning if momentum was to be retained and others drawn to the fold.

With its focus on intricate correlations of private and public experience 'Trip to Hanoi' shares some common ground with American 'new journalism' of the period, such as Norman Mailer's *The Armies of the Night* (1968). Sontag, like Mailer, is concerned to expose the narrative 'I' as a written construct and interrogate her own potentialities for understanding, but she does not share his confident presentation of selfhood or sense of a rite of passage fought for in the immediacy of experience. In a 1968 interview she comments: 'I'm just not temperamentally capable of using the kind of direct, immediate, first-person experience that Mailer uses in his essays.'[16] While 'Trip to Hanoi' does work to underline first-person experience it eschews Mailer's technical fireworks and sense of imperial selfhood. Sontag's fragmented, introspective commentary (facilitated in the first half of her text by a diary format) offers a much more intense form of self-reflection. The drama of her text lies in its movement towards a sense of self-discovery, implicating broader moral and political issues as she explores cultural difference and identity and asks how she can bridge not only the difference between Vietnamese and American but 'the difference between being an actor (them) and being a spectator (me)' (*SRW* 218).

The first half of 'Trip to Hanoi' focuses on the seemingly insurmountable cultural difference Sontag experiences in the first few days of the trip. She quickly comes to see that her 'bewilderment' was partly due to her 'lack of a purpose' in going to Vietnam; she had been invited as an 'American friend' (*SRW* 210), presumed (without question) to be committed to the Vietnamese cause. It is this very lack of a chosen role – in one sense, a clearly defined position of interpretation – that quickly brings home to her her 'ignorance' of Vietnamese culture and people, and ultimately helps her to approach the culture in a way that may not have been possible had she set out with the intention of writing on her experience. As she puts it near the beginning of her text: 'If occasionally I could have reminded myself that I was a writer and Vietnam was "material", I might have fended off some of the confusions that beset me' (*SRW* 206). Lacking this 'shield' of intention and point of view she enters into a confused state of cultural dislocation, immersing her reader in this dilemma. The reader should not be naive about this confusion, for clearly the experience of dislocation is structurally important to her text if the later relocation of self and the sense of Sontag having been changed by her experience are to have any impact.

Sontag's distance or detachment from the Vietnamese, her experience as a 'spectator', is partly expressed in the first section of her text as a result of the seeming uniformity of Vietnamese culture and language use. She is bemused when 'plied with gifts and flowers and rhetoric and tea' – the equivalent status of 'rhetoric' here implying an apparent sameness of language and action in Vietnam. Everything seems to be experienced, valued, and expressed at a surface level. The rituals of the Vietnamese she encounters keep her at a distance, and this includes ritualistic forms of speech. She finds that it is 'especially hard to see people as individuals … everybody here seems to talk in the same style and to have the same things to say' (*SRW* 213). What she finds most difficult in this respect is:

the stylising of language: speaking mostly in simple declarative sentences, making all discourse either expository or interrogative. Everything is on one level here. All the words belong to the same vocabulary; struggle, bombings, friend, aggressor, imperialist, patriot, victory, brother, freedom, unity, peace.

(SRW 216)

Sontag is uncomfortable with this language for it shows no signs of irony or self-consciousness; for her, as a postwar American radical the languages of nationalism and communism seem embarrassingly corrupt and unacceptable at face value. As she puts it; 'It's not that I judge their [the Vietnamese's] words to be false' but is it difficult to throw off 'the old conviction of the inadequacy of their language' (SRW 216).

This scepticism is not only formed by her radical American history though, for it is also an ingrained intellectual disposition which baulks at the 'naïveté' of such language use. The Vietnamese and their modes of expression are just not complex enough for her Western tastes – a point Sontag clearly wants to underline:

My consciousness, reared in [American] culture, is a creature with many organs, accustomed to being fed by irony. While I don't think I'm lacking in moral seriousness, I shrink from having my seriousness ironed out; I know I'd feel reduced if there were no place for its contradictions and paradoxes, not to mention its diversions and distractions. Thus, the gluttonous habits of my consciousness prevent me from being at home with what I most admire, and – for all my raging against America – firmly unite me to what I condemn. 'American friend' indeed! (SRW 223)

I live in an unethical society that coarsens the sensibilities and thwarts the capacities for goodness of most people but makes available for minority consumption an astonishing array of intellectual and aesthetic pleasures ... [I] can't deny the immense richness of these pleasures, or my addiction to them. (SRW 224)

This seems a disarming honesty on Sontag's part, and certainly a key concern of her writing this essay is to lay bare some of her most basic intellectual and cultural values. But she also wants to interrogate the limitations of these values and have her reader witness her efforts to transcend these limitations.

In the first half of 'Trip to Hanoi' Sontag's interpretation of

Vietnam and the Vietnamese has been clearly interest bound by her cultural and intellectual prejudices. The Vietnamese are found to be *non-Western*: their language *lacks* irony; their historical understanding *lacks* complexity; they are 'naive' and 'childlike' – in short, underdeveloped Westerners. They are found to be so because of the bias in her Western preoccupations and assumptions, which comes uncomfortably close to reflecting the most zealously ethnocentric prejudices about Vietnamese people and their culture. Sontag pursues this ethnocentric line in order that she can begin to unpick its prejudices and offer an alternative approach to Vietnam in the second half of her essay. This is not to deny that she means what she says about her 'addiction' to the West, she does, but as the text does not end here I believe that these findings may most usefully be read as a necessary foregrounding of how inescapable her Western consciousness is. Having established the complex nature of her American baggage she then goes on to reorient her approach to Vietnam.

At the beginning of the second section of 'Trip to Hanoi' Sontag drops her diary format and with it the intense subjective focus on her preoccupations, noting that these diary entries have conveyed 'the callowness and stinginess of my response' (*SRW* 234). She also notes that before visiting Vietnam her 'understanding of the country was limited to Vietnam's election as the target of what's most ugly in America: the principle of "will", the self-righteous taste for violence, the insensate prestige of technological solutions to human problems' (*SRW* 234). (These are precisely the views reflected in her statement on 'What's Happening in America'.) The mistake with this form of thinking is that it idealistically situates Vietnam as a victimised other of an American will to power; Vietnam has no identity or 'will' of its own, merely providing a reflection of American 'ugliness'. She makes a similar mistake once in Vietnam by conceptualising its people and culture as unselfconscious others to her self-conscious self and culture. It is only when the acuteness of this self-conscious response, its demanding double-perspectives, begins to relax and Sontag begins to consider 'the nature of Vietnamese will – its styles, its range, its nuances' (*SRW* 234) that she is able to move beyond the abstract nature of her early responses.

As she begins to adapt to her surroundings she contextualises what she hears and observes more concretely. She begins a careful examination of a number of Vietnamese cultural concepts, attempting to situate them in the contexts of Vietnamese history and social structures. She wants to draw out what is specifically Vietnamese about the connotations of, for example, 'respect', 'politeness', 'sincerity', 'cleanliness', 'suffering', and 'democracy'. Although she does not entirely eschew the synchronic approach of cross-cultural reference, this is either played down or more strictly controlled. She notes, for example, that 'respect' has complex moral connotations in Vietnamese society. The Vietnamese admiration of Norman Morrison, she eventually realises, is not a sentimental 'cult' but a recognition of 'the moral success of [Morrisons's] deed, its completeness, as an act of self-transcendence' (*SRW* 236). Therefore, she notes, the Vietnamese are *'speaking quite accurately* when they declare their "respect" for him and when they call him, as they often do, their "benefactor"' (*SRW* 236; emphasis added). Similarily, with 'sincerity' she locates specific Vietnamese values ascribed – 'personal dignity', 'shamelessness' – which only take on meaning when it is understood that the Vietnamese 'have a normative or prescriptive notion of sincerity', and so 'sincerity, in Vietnam, means behaving in a manner *worthy* of one's role; sincerity is a mode of ethical aspiration' (*SRW* 238). Sontag conducts a similar investigation of other terms, all the while working to situate these in Vietnamese contexts.

This is a more considered analysis of what she experienced during her first few days in Hanoi as a blandness and conformity in Vietnamese life and expression. Coming to view the lack of intellectual reflection and problematising as something other than 'naive' she wants to make Vietnamese 'matter-of-factness' credible. When she writes towards the end of her text that the Vietnamese 'lack both time and incentive for symbolic controversy' (*SRW* 256) the pejorative nature of this insight as it implicitly appeared in the first section has been dropped. In place of 'symbolic controversy' Sontag finds the Vietnamese privileging the instrumental and utilitarian; 'words are for use' (*SRW* 255) and language and ideas may be seen as indices of the more general frugality of a society making optimum use of every resource. She notes, for instance, that every component of American planes which have been shot down is put to some use: 'An unholy dialectic is at work here, in which the big wasteful society dumps its garbage', and the Vietnamese 'then go about picking up the debris, out of which they fashion materials for daily use and self-defence' (*SRW* 255).

The Vietnamese present Sontag with a very different style of 'radical will' from that of her Western contemporaries. Towards the end of her essay she turns the pragmatic lessons she has learned of

Vietnamese revolution against the most public forms of dissent in the West to suggest that Western radicalism is helplessly burdened by reflectiveness in the overtly symbolic forms it takes. Believing that 'talk' rather than more direct forms of 'feeling' characterises Western radicalism – the taste for 'symbolic controversy' she notes in herself – she argues that this disables the drive for real changes:

> What brings about genuine revolutionary change is the shared experience of revolutionary *feelings* – not rhetoric, not the discovery of social injustice, not even intelligent analysis, and not any action considered in itself. And one can indeed 'talk' revolutions away, by a disproportion between consciousness and verbalisation, on the one hand, and the amount of practical *will* on the other. (Hence the failure of the recent revolution in France. The French students talked – and very beautifully, too – instead of reorganising the administration of the captured universities. Their staging of street demonstrations and confrontations with the police was conceived as a rhetorical or symbolic, rather than a practical, act; it too was a kind of talking.) (*SRW* 263-264)

Curiously, this tendentious commentary is tucked away as a footnote, as if an aside to Sontag's main concerns – perhaps she felt that it needed (as it does) greater elaboration and support – but it is central to these concerns for it calls into question all styles of radical will which are symbolically oriented, from Jean Luc Godard to Abbie Hoffman, from the Living Theatre to the 1967 march on the Pentagon. In *The Armies of the Night* Norman Mailer treats the Pentagon march as a major symbolic challenge to state and corporate power. He observes the 'incredible spectacle now gathering – tens of thousands travelling hundreds of miles to attend a symbolic battle' and credits the radical young with creating a spectacle in which 'the aesthetic was at last in the politics'. What he admires in the young is their very lack of pragmatism in making and living the revolution: there is no great narrative of history giving meaning to events – indeed 'the history of the past was being exploded' – while the future is given over to chance as 'one's idea of a better existence would be found or not found in the context of the revolution'.[17] For Mailer, the aestheticisation of politics makes America a land of possibility once again – Mailer as jeremiad – while Sontag, confronting the alien 'practical will' of the Vietnamese, feels bound to question the symbolic will of Western radicalism as an instrument of major social change.

The distinction Sontag posits between a symbolic, reflective (American) will and an instrumental, practical (Vietnamese) will is partly a projection of a conflict within her own critical consciousness, a reflection of her effort to scrutinise her own radical will. This distinction would suggest that while she warns against constructing Vietnam as an 'ideal Other' (*SRW* 271) – as a means of focusing moral and political American issues – she nonetheless idealises the *silence* of Vietnam in her own highly aesthetic terms as a negation of Western selfhood. While she warns against framing psychological questions about the Vietnamese she does this herself, to produce some questionable speculations: 'The Vietnamese are "whole" human beings, not "split" as we are' (*SRW* 263). Sontag is not unaware of the risks of idealising the alterity of her subject. In her essay on Claude Lévi-Strauss in *Against Interpretation* she observes: 'Modern thought is pledged to a kind of applied Hegelianism: seeking its Self in its Other ... The "other" is experienced as a harsh purification of "self." But at the same time the "self" is busily colonising all strange domains of experience.' (*AI* 69-70). In 'Trip to Hanoi', as in so much of her writing, she wants to keep alive a sense of otherness and stay the predatory nature of interpretation. She tries to do this by foregrounding the failure of her consciousness and language to 'incorporate' (*SRW* 271) Vietnam, claiming that her experience there was in excess of interpretation – she leaves us with a sense of absence, of silence, mocking the limits of her culture and of her own thinking. While her thought processes and language use (for all her qualifications and use of parentheses) inevitably construct an imaginary Vietnam, she is also attuned to the ideological implications of projecting an unmediated communion with the totally other as a narcissistic embrace of her mirror image.[18]

At the end of her diary-essay Sontag registers some doubts and confusions about what to make of her experience in Vietnam beyond her certainty that it has forced her to confront the ideological closure of her own intellectual (American) outlook. She is reluctant to draw clear personal and political conclusions. She is not so naive as to ask for a return to innocence as this would be a corruption of her own terms of argument, and indeed she insists that 'the revolution that remains to be made [in America] must be made in American terms' (*SRW* 271). Vietnam, she contends, offers no blueprints for a revolution in America. However, she does suggest that the very otherness of Vietnam challenges American radicals to scrutinise the meanings of their intellectual alienation from their own country and transcend the limitations of their 'culture-bound' political imaginings. 'Trip to Hanoi' affirms such a change in consciousness as its author's *experience*. With typical self-consciousness, in the closing section of her text, Sontag recognises that 'anything really serious I'd gotten from my trip would return me to my starting point: the dilemmas of being an American, an unaffiliated radical American, an American writer' (*SRW* 271). Yet this restatement of awareness about the limitations and limiting nature of her language and consciousness is not the closing statement of her text. Rather she concludes with the affirmation that her experience in Vietnam has been a 'transformative' one in which 'new feelings' emerged and that with her return to the United states she is 'trying to make these feelings live here in an appropriate and authentic form' (*SRW* 273).

There is a logic to such an ending within the text of her 'interior journey' (*SRW* 270) in North Vietnam, and in the text of *Styles of Radical Will* as a whole. We should recognise that Sontag's repeated references to her 'experience' and 'feelings' in Vietnam (very deliberately set in opposition to and privileged over her preconceptions and overt intellectualising) carry phenomenological and transcendental emphases which echo those of her writings on aesthetics. In visiting Vietnam, she tells us, 'all things are thrown into question' including 'American attitudes' towards language, eros, and identity (*SRW* 271). In her analyses of 'silent' art works or certain works of the pornographic imagination she is similarly concerned with challenges to common attitudes and assumptions and the 'undoing' of selfhood. A fascination with the idea of self-transcendence is as apparent in 'Trip to Hanoi' as it is in the other essays in *Styles of Radical Will*. The difference is that where this idea had been conceived in the abstract when she theorised on the aesthetics of silence it is now presented to us as her personal experience, an experience made both difficult and necessary (she describes it as 'a pressing moral imperative' (*SRW* 273)) due to the historical and ideological conditions militating against it. This experience is no fanciful escape from the 'predatory embrace of consciousness' – certainly, it does not exist in the ontological vacuum she explores in *Death Kit*. Sontag refuses to patronise her 'new feelings'. Remarking, simply, that they are 'indelible' she ends her text: 'So I discover that what happened to me in North Vietnam did not end with my return to America, but is still going on' (*SRW* 274). The dialectics of self and other inscribed in her reflections on her journey offer no simple resolutions to the intellectual dilemmas she foregrounds, but they do lead her to a fresh synthesis of her aesthetic and political perspectives and to the intimation of a new mode of radical will.

I have dwelt on 'Trip to Hanoi' at some length as it represents a significant rethinking by Sontag of her aesthetic concerns and her first detailed effort to relate these to her political perspectives. In this text her critical views on left radicalism in the United States, more particularly her scepticism about the symbolic forms it takes, are generally low-key, often parenthetical. In a later travel essay, 'Some Thoughts on the Right Way (for us) to Love the Cuban Revolution' (1969), her criticisms are more detailed and polemically accented. In this shorter, more discursive essay she argues that the New Left's preoccupation with 'cultural revolution' and 'psychic redemption' is ideologically ensnared by its very Americanism:

> The new American radicalism is, I think, undeniably more intelligent and more sensitive and more creative than the so-called Old Left. But it is also, as part of these same virtues, more provincial, more excruciatingly American. If the main struggle at this moment is to establish an alternative or adversary culture, it is entirely American that that struggle flourishes around the goal of *freedom* (not, for instance, justice). And even more specifically American is what is understood as the content of freedom – the guarantee of freedom to the *individual*. American radicals are claiming one of the fundamental promises of American society – the promise to protect each person's right to non-participation, disaffiliation, selfishness.[19]

Sontag's complaint, spurred by her recognition of how differently the Cubans view their relation to their own 'majority culture' and to the 'imperial' American culture, is not with the ends of American radicals' revolutionary vision – 'our longing to participate in the creation of a new human nature' – but with the means, the 'mainly cultural warfare' which does not severely test the core values and beliefs of her society and which is quickly 'co-opted'.[20]

This critique of left radicalism is partly self-directed, for Sontag shares what she questions here as 'a very American attitude, which inclines toward a suspicion of all approved, official, majority culture', and must also ask herself why it is that 'American radicals can barely envisage a new role for intellectuals which goes beyond the traditional oppositional one.'[21] This traditional role is one that she has inherited and claims strong allegiance to (as we have seen from her comments on the role of the writer as a dissident voice), but her experience of travelling to these other cultures and witnessing the modes of radical will and intellectual inquiry there throws her back upon herself to question the legitimacy and functionalism of this role. In 'Trip to Hanoi' she speculates in a similar vein on the alienated, individualistic stance of Western radicals: 'Revolution in the Western capitalist countries seems, more often than not, to be an activity expressly designed never to succeed. For many people, it is an *a*social activity, a form of action designed for the assertion of individuality against the body politic. It is the ritual activity of outsiders' (*SRW* 264).

In writing such critical comments on counter-cultural and New Left radicalism Sontag cannot have been unaware that she was widely identified with the movement towards cultural and 'psychic revolution' by the late 1960s. Some part of her critical perspective here may be a response to that public identity, an effort to distance herself from 'the radicalization of hip'.[22] By the time she wrote her political travelogues the 'new sensibility' was a widely used phrase; referring not only to the perspectives of a handful of innovative artists and critics, it came to refer rather to a 'political-cultural sensibility' of a broad based 'adversary culture' devoted to radical changes in American society as well as in the arts. In *An Essay on Liberation* (1969) Herbert Marcuse describes the 'new sensibility' as 'the demand of the life instinct' to create 'a new type of man'. For Marcuse, this demand shows promise of realisation in the aesthetic elements of left radicalism, and he points with enthusiasm to 'the May rebellion in France' as 'the rebellion for the total transvaluation of values, for qualitatively different ways of life'.[23] In the early 1960s, as we have seen, Sontag sympathised with Marcuses's emphasis on the 'aesthetic sense' as a transcendent means of recognising the correspondences of 'eroticism and liberty' (*AI* 257). In 'The Pornographic Imagination' she could be said to carry this perspective into her argument that certain forms of pornographic literature fulfil the fantasy of self-negation and offer glimpses of alternative modes of consciousness not catered for by her society. In her essays on Vietnam and Cuba, however, she questions the aesthetic and symbolic strains within ideas of radical transvaluation and sets herself apart from Marcuse's utopianism.

Marcuse's concept of 'a new type of man' is an exemplary statement of the aesthetics of American radicalism in the late 1960s. Richard Poirier has observed that in the work of Marcuse, Norman

Mailer, and other left radicals of this period there is a form of pastoralism evident in their efforts to imagine 'a change in consciousness' as a prelude to a social revolution. He notes that Marcuse and Mailer locate what they perceive as the threatened human attributes of 'erotic energy, of freedom, and dignity' in the forms and activity of art: 'Thus art in Marcuse is called the "great negation", and in Mailer the very practice of art, of being a Novelist, is elevated to that of a hero ... Both are staunchly elitist.'[24] That Sontag is no less an elitist is readily evident in her attributing to 'serious art' the 'power to negate' and to 'satisfy the appetite for exalted self-transcending modes' of consciousness. Unlike Marcuse and Mailer, though, she cannot envisage a radical project of social change being based upon aesthetic principles. Where she most distinctly differs from these critics is in her reluctance to press the concept of artistic negation into a radical politics.

This reluctance is evident in Sontag's efforts in the late 1960s 'to incorporate' into her writings her 'evolving radical political convictions and sense of moral dilemma at being a citizen of the American empire'. Her struggle to square her aesthetic and political perspectives is limited by the rhetoric of modernism she utilises. The idea of transcendence she associates with the 'spiritual restlessness' of modernism is exemplified in the individual will of the artist or intellectual, not in the collective will of a political mass. An implication of her critique of counter-cultural and New Left thinking is a concern that the radical political correlative of the artistic myth of silence is a form of 'neo-primitivism', an anti-intellectual commitment to a 'psychic revolution'.[25] (In positing such a concern she echoes that of many Old Left New York intellectuals about the massification of avant-gardist ideas.) As we have seen, throughout her 1960s writings she debates with herself both the appeal and limitations of an 'aesthetic sensibility'. Where it holds considerable appeal for her in the early 1960s as a provocation to the liberal imagination, by the end of the decade she is very wary of 'overgeneralising the aesthetic view of the world' (SSR 331).

MELANCHOLY MEDITATIONS

From 1969 to 1972 Sontag lived a life of semi-exile from the United States, spending much of this time in Sweden where she directed two independent films.[1] In 1972, living in Paris, she found herself in what she would later describe as 'a great crisis':

> I'm in a tiny room in Paris thinking. Where am I? What have I done? I seem to have become an expatriate, but I didn't mean to become an expatriate. I don't seem to be a writer anymore, but I wanted most of all to be a writer. So I gave up a film project in Paris – I'd written the script and had the go-ahead from a small independent producer there – and began to write again.[2]

The writings she produced in the early and mid-1970s evidence repercussions of this crisis, of doubts about her ambitions and role as a writer–intellectual. She is even more intensely a theorist of her own sensibility in the 1970s as she seeks to reassess her aesthetic, moral, and political views and feelings in new contexts. When in the late 1960s she wrote with a 'sense of standing in the ruins of thought and on the verge of the ruins of history and of man himself', this was an apocalyptic sense of change and discovery. In the 1970s Sontag still pictures herself standing in these ruins, but now the tone is elegiac. The world she contemplates is frequently referred to as a 'posthumous' one all but voided of either intellectual belief or moral passion; it is also an interregnum, a crucial transitional time of cultural and personal redefinitions.

Sontag is not alone in her sense of intellectual crisis in the early 1970s as many American writers and intellectuals examined what was widely perceived as the diminishment of radical, utopian thinking and became increasingly dismayed at the paucity of public critical discourses. Writing in 1978 Elizabeth Hardwick articulated the shock of recognition experienced by many as the 'Sixties' became a historical memory:

> Only the forgetful can easily ignore the duplicity practised upon the defining imagination by the sudden obsolescence of attitudes and styles just past, styles that collapsed or scattered into fragments just as one had felt free to identify them as facts, changes, alterations of consciousness, shiftings of power or threats to power. These elements, at least at the moment of identification, had the shape of reality, of historical presence, of genuine displacements; and even though they could not be asserted as eternal they still could not be experienced as mere historical moments soon, very soon, to be reversed or simply erased. It is with some perturbation that one has to learn again and again that the power of external forces is greater than style, stronger than fleeting attitude.[3]

It is a lesson that much agitated New York intellectuals in the 1970s and was a defining feature of the debates which most engaged them: 'the crisis of liberalism', 'the triumph of the therapeutic', the 'culture of narcissism', and 'the cultural contradictions of capitalism'. Those New York intellectuals who still retained left-liberal sentiments feared a new alienation from political life, the collapse of a public sphere of political debate, and an increased conservatism in critical attitudes.[4]

While rarely directly addressing these debates in her 1970s writings Sontag constantly cuts across them or echoes them. She still ranges across diverse subjects, taking as her metasubject 'what it means to be modern', both as an individual critical temperament and as a general cultural condition. However, contemporary modernism attracts her less and she very deliberately distances herself from what she sees as the easy commercial incorporation of modernist energies. Her two major essay collections in this period, *Under the Sign of Saturn* (1980) and *On Photography* (1977), may seem to have little in common at first glance but both effect this distancing while reaffirming the need for critical, creative thinking. She resists the claims of a radically new 'postmodern' culture in favour of examining what remains of the modernist tradition – of its asceticism and powers of negation – at a time when it has been 'stripped … of its claims as an adversary sensibility' (*USS* 138). One consequence of this is that the elegiac note always present in her writing is strengthened, brought to the fore, as she goes about ruminating among the ruins of that tradition.

The life of the mind

The essays gathered in *Under the Sign of Saturn* are studies, or 'portraits' (Sontag's preferred term), of highly individual artists and thinkers: Paul Goodman, Antonin Artaud, Leni Riefenstahl, Walter Benjamin, Hans Jürgen Syberberg, Roland Barthes, and Elias Canetti. Taken collectively the essays propose a fractured counter-tradition of modernist thought. But this is also a very personal collection, focused by the author's desire to pay homage to particular infuences and preoccupations. Indeed, one of the subtexts of the collection is an inquiry into what it means to admire powerful artistic and intellectual models (with Riefenstahl very much the cuckoo in the nest of Sontag's admirations). Sontag admires the ways her subjects variously champion 'the life of the mind', reflecting her interest in dramaturgies of thought and the lived experience of demanding intellectual vocations. Leo Braudy is correct to suggest that the essays establish and celebrate 'a genealogy of mind'.[5] We may recognise defining features of this genealogy in Sontag's inference that most of her subjects show signs of a 'melancholic temperament' and that they project themselves onto their subjects; in their projects she recognises various forms of self-assemblage, the self on display within the work. These issues of melancholia and self-display are related for Sontag: self-awareness, the problematics of thinking about thinking, and the locating of being in thinking, these are the melancholic's subject she argues and the linking thematic in *Under the Sign of Saturn*.

Sontag views most of her subjects as inaugurators of artistic and intellectual projects which carry the mark of a Romantic-cum-modernist amibition to create what she variously terms the 'Great Work' or 'total' work. She provides her most expansive description at the beginning of her essay on Syberberg where she notes how the concept of the 'masterpiece' shifted from the Romantic valorisation of 'heroism, a breaking through or going beyond' to the more extreme claims on the modernist to provide something 'terminal or prophetic, or both' (*USS* 137). The modernist Great Work, she observes, 'proposed satisfactions that are immense, solemn, and restricting. It insists that art must be true, not just interesting; a necessity, not just an experiment. It dwarfs other work, challenges the facile eclecticism of contemporary taste. It throws the admirer into a state of crisis' (*USS* 138). Sontag has used such terminology before. In *Against Interpretation*, for example, she refers to modernist writers 'who close off rather than inaugurate, who cannot be learned from, so much as imitated' (AI 102); and in several of the essays in *Styles of Radical Will* she shows her respect for 'serious art' as 'a deliverance, an exercise in asceticism' (*SRW* 8). There is, though, something more defiant and willed in this later, more sustained appraisal of the modernist ambition above, a determination at least to celebrate it as against the grain of a contemporary 'facile eclecticism', which hints at a disappointment in her contemporaries and (though this is much clearer in her essays on photography) a pessimism about the supposed gains of avant-gardism in the 1960s.

Sontag's interest in the flawed but ambitious intellectual project is clearly present in the lead essay in *Under the Sign of Saturn*, 'On Paul Goodman' (1972). This short piece, seemingly little more than an affectionate memoir, contains a number of the related themes noted above which run throughout the volume. The first thing the reader notices is the somewhat tense self-conscious opening which has us imagine the writer 'writing this in a tiny room in Paris, sitting on a wicker chair at a typing table in front of a window which looks onto a garden; at my back is a cot and a night table; on the floor and under the table are manuscripts, notebooks, and two or three paperback books' (*USS* 3). This introduction reveals a writer trying to ground herself and the reader, to make a beginning; we sense that she needs to very deliberately write herself into the text and the rather mechanical description of the room seems to serve this function. We are then told she had 'some need to strip down, to close off for a while, to make a new start with as little as possible to fall back on' (*USS* 3). The bareness of her surroundings is so described to suggest the desire for disburdenment she admits to feeling only vaguely, and we may recognise this as a literalisation of the fantasies of disburdenment present in much of Sontag's work. It seems to be a desire for a personal clean slate, to 'live and work' as unburdened as possible by either social communication or intellectual stimulation (we note how few books there are in the room) in an effort 'to hear my own voice and discover what I really think and feel' (*USS* 10). It also marks the introduction of the theme on melancholy, though this is not specifically mentioned, but isolation and self-interrogation are clearly identified in later essays as marks of the melancholic.

There is also in her emphasis on hearing her 'own voice' and discovering what she 'really' thinks and feels an intimation of authenticity, of trying to locate something essential. Notably, she gives weight to certain details which establish for her the inviolable character or individuality of those she is studying. With Goodman the detail is his voice: 'It was that voice that seduced me – that direct, cranky, egotistical, generous American voice' (*USS* 6). As with the other essays she quite deliberately focuses on a specific detail which, although it may be developed into a quite broad analysis of the writer, limits her interest and concerns. She identifies with Goodman's voice in the sense that it denotes a 'breadth of moral passion' and characterises the nature of his intellectual project, its 'amateurism' (*USS* 8). She recognises Goodman as an intellectual generalist and there is more than a hint of self-interest in her observation that: 'There is a terrible, mean American resentment toward a writer who tries to do many things' (*USS* 7). Clearly identifying with the free-ranging and non-systematic nature of Goodman's writings Sontag offers a retort to his detractors: '[Goodman's] so-called amateurism is identical with his genius: that amateurism enabled him to bring to the questions of schooling, psychiatry, and citizenship an extraordinary, curmudgeonly accuracy of insight and freedom to envisage practical change' (*USS* 8). This intellectual range both signifies the modernist ambition of Goodman – a variant on the theme of the Great Work – and the inevitable failure which comes of trying 'to do almost everything a writer can do' (*USS* 8).

Sontag posits a similarly ambitious failure in her essay on Antonin Artaud, finding that the diversity and range of his writings and projects 'amount to a broken ... corpus, a vast collection of fragments' (*USS* 17). She views all his 'ventures inspired by the ideal of a total art form' which will overcome dualisms (mind and body, conscious and unconscious) and tap a plenitude of Being with a spatial language of performance. Such a project must fail for the reason Sontag points out in *Styles of Radical Will* (and dramatises somewhat ironically in *Death Kit*): to deny dualism is to deny consciousness and plot a path to madness, asphasia, or silence. But it is the *ambition* she is interested in and the most striking feature of her essay is its concentration on the excesses of Artaud's life and writings in an effort to dramatise the 'ordeal' of a 'consciousness *in extremis'* (*USS* 66-7). In this she deliberately avoids any effort to assess his writings, but rather focuses on what they tell us of his own self-alienation. The focus on Artaud's 'pain' and its presence in his work is sanctioned in part by her belief that his work should not be interpreted, that indeed it resists interpretation. She ends the essay with the argument that Artaud is 'unusable' – 'he remains fiercely out of reach, an unassimilable voice and presence' (*USS* 70) – refusing any effort to systematise his thought as a poetics of theatrical production and performance.

In her essays on Canetti and Barthes Sontag is less strenuously 'against interpretation', though again she focuses selectively on particular elements of temperament and characteristics of their ambitious intellectual projects. Canetti is presented as a 'placeless' intellectual, an 'exile' with an 'intellectual insatiability' which cannot be appeased. As with Goodman, she identifies with the polymath nature of Canetti's interests and writings and his 'passionate but also acquisitive relations to knowledge and truth' (*USS* 187). In her short essay on Barthes (another elegiac memoir) she celebrates yet another intellectual who 'wrote about everything' (*USS* 172), but one with a temperament more ludic and 'amorous' than the others she admires. She describes him as a 'voluptuary of the mind' (*USS* 176-7) and 'a taxonomist of jubilation' (*USS* 170). A longer essay on Barthes, 'Writing Itself: On Roland Barthes' (1981, this essay does not appear in *Under the Sign of Saturn*) picks up this theme – Barthes-as-aesthete – to argue that his emphases on pleasure, desire, multiplicity of meaning, and antithetical thinking are constituents of an aesthetic way of viewing the world. For Sontag, Barthes's aesthetic perspective is at one with his 'immensely complex enterprise of self-description' (*USS* 173); it is an enterprise which 'constitutes the self as the locus of all possibilities, avid, unafraid of contradiction … a vision of the life of the mind as a life of desire, of full intelligence and pleasure' (*SSR* 444).

Among all these admiring portraits it is the essay on Benjamin, notably the title essay in *Under the Sign of Saturn*, that most fully delineates the metatheme of melancholic self-description. Temperament again provides a focus for Sontag's approach, as she proposes that Benjamin's 'temperament determined what he chose to write about' (*USS* 111), constantly drawing him to find interest in the marginalised, the overlooked, the seemingly banal. Benjamin's relation to 'the life of the mind' is not Artaud's 'carnal' spontaneity, nor Barthes's sensual avidity, but rather a low-key, introspective 'mapping' of one's relation to the world. Sontag responds to his spatial form of understanding which is expressed in 'the recurrent metaphors of labyrinths and arcades, vistas and panoramas' (*USS* 112), and to his preference for turning 'the flow of events into a tableau' (*USS* 115-16). What she is drawn to and explores in this essay is the relationship between Benjamin's famous melancholic temperament and his convoluted means of engaging the world and history – an understanding of history, Benjamin proposes, is 'a process of empathy whose origin is indolence of the heart, acedia' (*USS* 164). Benjamin is portrayed as a writer obsessed with 'the melancholic's labours of decipherment' which are characterised by 'slowness', 'secretiveness', 'concentration', and 'allegorisation'.

This correspondence between temperament and style in the melancholic intellectual is one Sontag had alluded to in one of her earliest essays – 'The Anthropologist as Hero' (1963) – on Claude Lévi-Strauss. Portraying Lévi-Strauss as a hubristic witness to the violent accretions of history, she criticises his structuralist practice of translating his subject 'into a purely formal code' yet argues that his 'extreme formalism and intellectual agnosticism are played off against an immense but thoroughly subdued pathos' (*AI* 80). The pathos is that of the anthropologist as a prime modernist, a solitary figure among the ruins of the sad tropics, 'submitting to the melancholy spectacle of the crumbling prehistoric past' (*AI* 73). The 'complex modern pessimism' Sontag associates with Lévi-Strauss's melancholic perspective is present but more darkly shaded in Benjamin's morbidity. 'Modernity', Benjamin writes, 'must be under the sign of suicide, an act which seals a will ... It is *the* achievement of modernity in the realm of passions' (*USS* 132). Allegory is a privileged mode of interpretation for the death – haunted melancholic, a means of decoding the ruins of history and of the present. In Benjamin's interest in fragments and ruins Sontag detects a strong affinity with the Surrealist tendency

> to generalise with ebullient candor the baroque cult of ruins; to perceive that the nihilistic energies of the modern era make everything a ruin or fragment – and therefore collectable. A world whose past has become (by definition) obsolete, and whose present churns out instant antiques, invites custodians, decoders, and collectors. (*USS* 120)

As a 'process which extracts meaning from the petrified and insignificant' (*USS* 124-5) allegory offers a means of spatialising and mapping such a posthumous world.

Sontag's essay is a highly selective treatment of Benjamin. It is easy enough to recognise her admiration for a melancholic who desires to keep 'his many "positions" open: the theological, the Surrealist/aesthetic, the communist' (*USS* 133), but there are many who would find complaint with this portrait, especially those who would want to see a much greater acknowledgement of his Marxist credentials.[6] Sontag is neither unaware of nor embarrassed about such selectivity, describing her portrait of Benjamin as 'an invention, a construction ... To single out the melancholy element in his temperament is obviously limiting, but that's what I identify with.'[7] This process of identification is the genesis and true subject of the essays in *Under the Sign of Saturn*. That the essay on Benjamin is such a self-conscious 'invention, a construction' is indicated in part by the peculiarly reflective way in which she presents him to her reader. The essay begins:

> In most of the portrait photographs he is looking down, his right hand to his face. The earliest one I know shows him in 1927 – he is thirty-five – with dark curly hair over a high forehead, mustache above a full lower lip: youthful, almost handsome. With his head lowered, his jacketed shoulders seem to start behind his ears; his thumb leans against his jaw; the rest of the hand, cigarette between bent index and third fingers, covers his chin; the downward look through his glasses – the soft, daydreamer's gaze of the myopic – seems to float off to the lower left of the photograph.   (*USS* 109)

This opening paragraph is followed by three others which focus on different photographs of Benjamin. Sontag is doing more than introducing the theme of melancholia. She is reflecting Benjamin's own interest in finding points of departure in minutiae, in detailed, almost microscopic attention to what may seem trivial. She is also attempting to identify a unique presence; in a sense the essay springs from reflection on the photographs, an effort to transmit the presence she responds to, to draw the person out of the photograph.

Shadowing Sontag's highly selective treatment of her subjects is her self-conscious attention to the essay form. Benjamin, Canetti, and Barthes she counts as exemplary practitioners of 'short forms', of the essay, aphorism, and fragmented discourse. Benjamin, she notes, viewed his essays as careful, labyrinthine 'reflections' upon their subjects. Even in her essay on Syberberg's film *Hitler* she describes the film as a kind of essay in which the lead voices 'ruminate' or 'meditate' on Hitler; it is a film of 'ruminations, images, associations, emotions connected with, evoked by, Hitler' (*USS* 158). 'Reflection' or 'rumination' are useful terms to characterise the Sontag essays we have been looking at as they suggest a personal element and a provisionality and partiality of treatment.[8] That Sontag shares her subjects' spaces we have already seen as she attempts to transmit as much as translate something of their 'agon' in her portraits. Thought in the essays is described and presented as alive, animated. In the essays on Artaud and Canetti, in particular, thought is a tangible essence, that which is coveted and longed for yet which distresses, estranges, or is out of control – for Artaud the mind is 'a physical substance that is intransigent, fugitive, unstable, obscenely mutable' (*USS* 18). The repeated emphasis on 'the life of the mind' throughout the essays identifies the animation of ideas while Sontag works to effect such animation, as in her flamboyant descriptions of Artaud's struggles to create, or in her dramatisation of the melancholic undertow in Benjamin's writings. The interrelationship between form and content in these essays is striking, and with the formal ploys by which she dramatises intersubjectivity – such as her opening reflections upon the photographs of Benjamin or her framing of the writer in the essay on Goodman – the boundaries between writer and critic become blurred.

Sontag's dramatisation of ideas unleashes a number of tensions, even contradictions, in her treatment of certain issues. There is a running debate within and between the essays on questions of aestheticism and (Romantic) individualism; the latter, as we have seen, a major theme, focused by her interest in the presence, uniqueness, and over-reaching nature of her subjects. But her celebration of 'the life of the mind' fails to unify issues thrown up, and assumptions which allow her to privilege this focus threaten to deconstruct. This issue may be usefully approached by turning to the essays on Leni Riefenstahl, 'Fascinating Fascism' (1974), and Hans Jürgen Syberberg, 'Syberberg's Hitler' (1979).

'Fascinating Fascism' is rightly celebrated as a highly effective interrogation of Riefenstahl's aesthetic philosophy and the mythology she helped build up around her own and her work's history. Quoting from the introduction to *The Last of the Nuba* (a 'ravishing book of photographs' by Riefenstahl, recently published), from Riefenstahl's own text on her prewar work, and from interviews,

Sontag carefully takes apart the myth of Riefenstahl as the put-upon German film maker who worked against the wishes of Goebbels. Sontag's attack is not confined to a marshalling of contextual sources, for she goes on to argue that all of Riefenstahl's work, from her early feature films to her Nazi propaganda films to the later photography, are 'fascist visuals'. In this reading, the early features are 'an anthology of proto-Nazi sentiments', and the recurrent action of mountain climbing 'a visually irresistible metaphor for unlimited aspiration toward the high mystic goal, both beautiful and terrifying' (USS 76); 'the mountain is represented as both supremely beautiful and dangerous, that majestic force which invites the ultimate affirmation of and escape from the self into the brotherhood of courage and into death' (USS 77). In the documentaries, Triumph of the Will (1935, on the Nuremberg rally of 1934) and Olympia (1938, on the Olympic games of 1936) Sontag identifies similar celebrations of the body, power, and discipline. With The Last of the Nuba she further asserts the 'continuity of the political and aesthetic ideas' (USS 97) in Riefenstahl's work, noting Riefenstahl's concentration on the athletic beauty of Nuba men and 'their proud heroic community' (USS 88). In extolling a 'primitivist ideal' Riefenstahl reflects a fascist 'contempt for all that is reflective, critical, and pluralistic' (USS 89).

Sontag's argument against Riefenstahl (and 'fascist aesthetics' more generally) calls into question her handling of key themes in Under the Sign of Saturn. The main problem that 'Fascinating Fascism' exposes is that she is unable to convincingly argue the dangers of one aspect of Romantic individualism while embracing another. Throughout these essays she praises the Great Work and especially its Romantic aspirations: the overpowering, the inaccessible, the awe-inspiring, the work that 'throws the admirer into crisis'. Similar vocabulary is used to describe Riefenstahl's films: the early features 'are about the vertigo before power' (USS 87), while the documentaries have to do with singleness of passion and ecstasy. In her essay on Canetti Sontag claims, following Canetti, that we should learn to 'breathe' as the end of admiration, where to breathe is to take in the rarefied air of the great work which 'both excites and paralyses the imagination' (USS 203). It may be that Sontag wants to identify the dangers of these Romantic impulses and has deliberately placed 'Fascinating Fascism' within Under the Sign of Saturn to suggest what may happen when admiration is not held in a state of 'crisis' but spills over into a mindless celebration of power. But while she excoriates Riefenstahl for promoting a fascist aesthetic she does little to question the politics of artistic self-aggrandisement elsewhere. Although she does comment on the 'anti-political' nature of Artaud's work she does not question the *politics* of his themes of transcendence and longing, of the 'emotional violence' of his ideal theatre, of his desire to immerse the audience in 'spectacle', of his following 'the romantic imperative to close the gap between art (and thought) and life' (*USS* 29). Although in 'Fascinating Fascism' she seems to want to identify a difference of ends depending on conception and context, her use of similar vocabulary to describe means opens up many more questions than she answers.

The essay on Riefenstahl reflects upon the other essays more uncomfortably than Sontag could have wished. In dealing with a real external world of power in this essay we recognise all the more the limiting treatment of interior worlds in her essays on Goodman, et al. Moreover, the question needs to be asked what kind of admiration or intellectual appreciation is it that she calls 'breathing' and how is it differentiated from that which fascist art encourages? The end of 'Fascinating Fascism' provides an oblique answer. Sontag suggests that 'the ironies of pop sophistication' (*USS* 95) permit detached aesthetic appreciation of the films and photographs. She makes it clear that what she is calling into question here is 'the sensibility of Camp, which is unfettered by the scruples of high seriousness' (*USS* 97). This would seem to be a sharp rejection of the camp perspective, but she immediately clouds this by stating:

> Art that seemed eminently worth defending ten years ago, as a minority or adversary taste, no longer seems defensible today, because the ethical and cultural issues it raises have become serious, even dangerous, in a way they were not then. The hard truth is that what may be acceptable in elite culture may not be acceptable in mass culture, that tastes which pose only innocuous ethical issues as the property of a minority become corrupting when they become more established.
>
> (*USS* 98)

On the one hand, Sontag seems to be calling into question (her own?) camp 'taste' but, on the other, protecting it by establishing a crude hierarchy of elite and mass cultures. As for the question of what kinds of admiration or appreciation she seems to be distinguishing between in these essays, it would seem that fascist art is not for the connoisseur who would 'breathe'.

I want to come at the relation between the aesthetic and the political from one further perspective by looking at the essay on Syberberg's film *Hitler*. In concordance with a key theme of *Under the Sign of Saturn* Sontag views *Hitler* as a modernist Great Work, believing that Syberberg has brought off 'a masterpiece' despite the familiarity of his subject and his romantic grandiosity of scope and aims. He succeeds, she believes, largely due to his modernist irony and self-reflexive use of cinema: 'Syberberg offers a spectacle about spectacle: evoking "the big show" called history in a variety of dramatic modes' (*USS* 138-9). *Hitler* knows itself to be a spectacle but also treats history as a form of spectacle – everything is a stand-in for the real. Quotation and assemblage are significant foregrounded features: quotation of cinema history; multiple voices on the sound track (including Hitler, Himmler, Goebbels, wartime news broadcasts, snatches of Wagner and Beethoven) interrelating with those of the actors; shifting images appear behind the actors, while the actors play several roles. That characters are themselves stand-ins for the real is underlined by having puppets and mannequins play a number of roles. As in her essays on Benjamin and Barthes, Sontag views this artist's self-conscious treatment of his medium as indicative of a 'posthumous' sensibility: a Surrealist eclecticism is at work which 'assumes a broken or posthumous world' (*USS* 145); everything is second hand, allegorical. The film signifies an effort by Syberberg to use his subject up: the film's recycling of quotations and images is described as 'pastiche', the film mimicking Wagnerian grandiosity.

The reader is clearly intended to opt for Syberberg's treatment of Hitler in preference to Riefenstahl's. Syberberg is the late-twentieth-century knowing conjurer of images, sceptical of the mediated nature of all forms of representation or historical understanding. In this he seems very different from Riefenstahl, who advances a fascist 'contempt for all that is reflective, critical, and pluralistic'. But this seems much too neat a packaging and juxtaposing of these film maker's credentials and impulses. Once again Sontag seems to posit, if only implicitly, a hierarchy of elite and mass: the directness and sentimentality of Riefenstahl is no match for the reflexivity and irony of Syberberg. And once again she loads the terms of her analysis by refusing to ask the historical and political questions of Syberberg that she asks of Riefenstahl. Firstly, she ignores how Syberberg manipulates his viewers: while she forces the question of political control on Riefenstahl as director she foists only that of aesthetic control on Syberberg – at no point does she consider how to draw the line between each form of control.[9] Secondly, and clearly related to the above point, she does not query what kind of historical understanding Syberberg presents. His fragmenting, quotations, and pastiche could be said to so distance or derealise history as to make it meaningless, a postmodern funhouse of voices and mirrors.

The manner in which Sontag loads her analysis in favour of Syberberg reflects upon the nature of her project in *Under the Sign of Saturn*. When she comments that he withdraws events from reality and restages them in 'the ideal theatre of the mind' (*USS* 157), she is dealing again with that interior world, 'the life of the mind', which so dominates the text. In these essays the melancholic mind promotes a 'self-conscious and unforgiving relation to the self, which can never be taken for granted' (*USS* 117). It is no surprise that Sontag celebrates irony, fragmentation, and uncertainty – the keynote of these essays is irresolution. The Great Works or intellectual projects are incomplete (Benjamin's deciphering and mapping are always ongoing; Syberberg's method is 'contradiction, irony'; Barthes's paradox and suspended meaning), while the admirer hovers in the state of admiration: 'The last achievement of the serious admirer is to stop immediately putting to work the energies aroused, by filling up the space opened by, what is admired' (*USS* 203-4). What else could the admiring essayist produce but provisional, partial, incomplete 'portraits'? Stability is spurned, though not lightly for it is viewed as dangerous, figured in this text as the submission to power Riefenstahl's work represents and evokes.

The state of irresolution characterises the individuality of those 'under the sign of Saturn'. It is clearly intended to characterise that of Sontag too, as my earlier comments on the form of her essay writing would suggest. She is a key presence in the essays, meditating on her subjects, and it is perhaps fitting that this is a revealing process. Sontag's own 'interminable self-definition of the self' (*USS* 117) is here poised in relation to and (agonistically) tested against that of other intellectuals, in what is a concentrated 'mapping' of her own interior, intellectual world. Sontag clearly believes in 'the mind as passion', that 'thought is a kind of excess', but while the essays are remarkable intersubjective exercises in admiration she occupies the space of her subjects more closely than she may be aware, for she is caught up in the problematic Romantic empowering of the individual and the aesthetic. We see Sontag's Romantic and high modernist credentials and biases on full display in these essays: the 'alienation' of the intellectual verges on a self-glorification of an outsider status.

It is worth noting that there is something willed in Sontag's idealisation of 'the life of the mind'. If, for example, Syberberg's film seems something of a 'retrograde feat, a naive form of accomplishment' at a time when modernism has been 'stripped of its heroic stature, of its claims as an adversary sensibility' (USS 138), then something similar may be said of *Under the Sign of Saturn* itself, at least in terms of Sontag's unabashed celebration of the intellectual outsider and the over-reaching artist. *Under the Sign of Saturn* is a perverse, private effort to keep the dead alive, to even revitalise the ambition which 'insists that art must be true, not just interesting' (USS 138). What she valorises as the authentic style and phenomenological experience of her chosen's works and worlds is what in 'The Aesthetics of Silence' she termed 'a standard of decorum' set by absolutist aspirations of modernist art. Where in the earlier essay she asserts that such aspirations must fail, in *Under the Sign of Saturn* – still acknowledging the inevitability of failure, knowing that as a secular form of religion the history of modernism is bestrewn with false idols – she celebrates what are for her some of the most 'heroic failures'. It is one of the ironies of her enterprise that she should try to salvage Romantic 'grandiosity' from the disrepute it has fallen into as camp or kitsch.

In *Under the Sign of Saturn* narcissism and nostalgia are bound up in Sontag's melancholy reflections on the decline of modernist ambitions. Her effort to do justice to her admirations presents her as both mourner and custodian of these ambitions. As in several of her 1960s writings, she comes close to what has been described as the postmodernist concern in mourning 'the shattered fantasy of the (always already) lost organic society that has haunted the Western imagination'.[10] Metaphorics of death, loss, and ecstasy circulate around her focus on melancholy, signifying both a nostalgia for and a departure from fantasies of plenitude, totality, unity, and mastery – those she admires are all 'destroyer[s] of … the consoling notion of the universally human' (USS 131). An alternative form of consolation is sought: it is the sufficiency of intellect she celebrates in the solitary figures (heroes of the will all) prospecting among the ruins of modernity.

Against photography

Between 1973 and 1977 Sontag published a series of essays on photography in the *New York Review of Books*; in 1977 six of these essays, in revised form, were published under the title *On Photography*. The essays do not represent a new interest in photography, though they present her first sustained and detailed commentaries on the subject. In earlier writings, particularly in her fiction, there are many scattered references to photography. Melancholia and morbidity are linked to several of the most interesting references. In *The Benefactor* one of her characters announces: 'Life is a movie. Death is a photograph' (B 182). The link between death and photography is one she returns to in her preface to the photographer Peter Hujar's *Portraits in Life and Death*, where she states: 'Photography converts the whole world into a cemetery. Photographers, connoisseurs of beauty, are also – wittingly or unwittingly – the recording-angels of death. The photograph-as-photograph shows death. More than that, it shows the sex-appeal of death.'[11] There are echoes of this idea in *On Photography*, both in Sontag's interest in the pathos of photographs and her treatment of photography as a predatory act, but this text goes well beyond such speculations to produce a highly ambitious reading of aesthetic, moral, and political implications of 'photographic seeing'.

In her preface to *On Photography* Sontag comments on the genesis of the essays: 'It all started with one essay – about some of the problems, aesthetic and moral, posed by the omnipresence of photographed images; but the more I thought about what photographs are, the more complex and suggestive they became. So one generated another.' This statement comments on both the scope and style of her essays. In a 1978 interview she describes photography as: 'a distinctly modern activity. Not just because it was invented in what we call the modern age, but because it incorporates and is the vehicle of all sorts of modern attitudes and ways of perceiving.'[12] Part of the attraction of writing on photography is that it allows her to reflect on 'what it means to be modern' and exercise her generalising instincts. As William Gass observes in his review of the text, the essays 'are not really about individual photographers, nor solely about the art, but rather about the act of photography at large, the plethora of the product, the puzzle of its nature'.[13] In these essays the movement from the specific to the general falls under the aegis of the contemplative intellect ('the more I thought about what

photographs are, the more complex and suggestive they became').
On Photography is, as Gass observes, 'a thoughtful meditation, not
a treatise'; it features digressive, circular arguments, making
numerous passes at its subject.[14]

It is also a text of surprising intellectual passion, studded with
provocative aphorisms and generalisations. It is, ultimately, a *moral*
disquisition on the omnipresence of photographed images. 'In
teaching us a new visual code', Sontag writes at the beginning of her
text, 'photographs alter and enlarge our notions of what is worth
looking at and what we have a right to observe. They are a grammar
and, even more importantly, an ethics of seeing' (*OP* 3). Throughout these essays she exhibits considerable moral perplexity about
what she views as disquieting aspects of photographed images. A
major theme, upon which many variations are sounded, is her concern about the 'predatory' nature of photography. A distinctive
vocabulary of keywords becomes apparent as we read: photography,
in this text, 'appropriates', 'violates', 'controls', 'distorts', 'anaes-
thetises', 'distances', 'captures', 'collects', and 'colonises'. This concern
with how photography acts upon the real in a predatory or acquisitive way weaves through all the essays, connecting diverse ideas and
arguments.

Sontag contends that photography has an adverse effect on
historical understanding because it abstracts and fragments; in historical terms, it destroys or at least encourages ignorance of context,
the lived history in which events first took on meaning. Her charge
that photography 'aestheticises' or 'beautifies' is not one levelled
against specific photographers so much as against the medium itself:
'Aesthetic distance', she notes, 'seems built into the very experience
of looking at photographs' (*OP* 21). Among several examples she
offers is that of W. Eugene Smith's late 1960s photographs of Japa-
nese fisherpeople in the village of Minamata who were suffering
and dying of mercury poisioning. While noting that these photographs 'move us because they document a suffering which arouses
our indignation', she also claims that they 'distance us because they
are superb photographs of Agony, conforming to surrealist stand-
ards of beauty' (*OP* 105). The photographs are dehistoricised and
depoliticised as they accord less with a lived history than with a
metaphysical, abstract state of being. 'One of the central characteristics of photography', Sontag writes, 'is that process by which
original uses are modified, eventually supplemented by subsequent
uses – most notably, by the discourse of art into which any photo-

graph can be absorbed' (*OP* 106). The meaning of a photograph cannot be secure; its plurality, relativity, and aesthetic relation to its subject will militate against any specific moral or political intentions.

In the second essay of *On Photography*, 'America, Seen Through Photographs, Darkly', Sontag reads these ideas of aesthetic transfiguration and 'neutralisation' into American photographic history to argue that they are the correlatives of a humanist ideology which she finds shadowing many photographic projects. Positing Walt Whitman as a key progenitor of this humanism in his vision of recording 'in its entirety the extravagant candors of actual American experience' (*OP* 29), she goes on to argue that his vision has been progressively corrupted in photographic practice. She views, for example, Walker Evans's photographs of Southern sharecroppers and their environments in the 1930s as 'levelling' in effect, that is levelling 'discriminations between the beautiful and the ugly, the important and trivial. Each thing or person photographed becomes, therefore, morally equivalent to any other of his photographs' (*OP* 30-1). If she finds Evans trying to affirm Whitman's programme she observes that with post-World War Two American photography 'the Whitmanian mandate ... has gone sour' (*OP* 29). A particular lowpoint, she suggests, is Edward Steichen's famous 'Family of Man' exhibition of 1955 which 'assumes a human condition or a human nature shared by everybody' and so 'denies the determining weight of history – of genuine and historically embedded differences, injustices, and conflicts' (*OP* 33). Sontag comes up to her present time of writing with a lengthy critique of Diane Arbus's photography. Recognising that Arbus's photographs of freaks and grotesques offer an 'anti-humanist message' she finds that no less than Steichen's her work renders 'history and politics irrelevant', due to her 'dissociated point of view' and 'atomising [of the human condition] into horror' (*OP* 33). Whitman's programme has been reduced to absurdity: 'Instead of showing identity between things which are different (Whitman's democratic vista), everybody is shown to look the same' (*OP* 47).

Sontag's second major complaint with 'photographic seeing' – clearly related to her views on aesthetic transfiguration and equivalence – is that 'the camera makes everyone a tourist in other people's reality, and eventually in one's own' (*OP* 57). The metaphor of tourism recurs in her text. It is introduced in the first essay where she notes that mass tourism has developed 'in tandem' with photography and points to several connections between the activities of travelling and taking photographs. Photographs 'help people to take possession of space in which they are insecure' (*OP* 9): travel photographs act as defences against anxiety, against the socio-geographic anxiety of dislocation, and the epistemological anxiety of needing to verify what is seen – make it real by photographing it. The tourism metaphor appears again in her examination of the middle-class origins of documentary photography where she derides the 'social adventurism' of treating 'reality as an exotic prize to be tracked down and captured by the diligent hunter-with-a-camera' (*OP* 54-5). The camera 'colonises' reality, yet detaches the viewer from the subject viewed. The camera makes us 'tourists' of reality by setting up 'a chronic voyeuristic relation to the world' (*OP* 11) which makes it unnecessary for us to feel personally involved in what we see.

One of the seeming paradoxes – it is presented as a paradox, which invites speculation – Sontag comes at again and again is that 'the medium which conveys distress ends by neutralising it' (*OP* 109). Her formulation of this paradox and speculations upon it indicate her anxiety about the effects of photographic images on capacities of moral response and historical understanding. This anxiety is made explicitly contemporary in the final essay, 'The Image World', which pulls together many ideas from preceding essays. Views already established on the aesthetic distancing and chronic voyeurism of photographic seeing now take on a broad socio-political import:

> Our unlimited use of photographic images not only reflects but gives shape to [American] society, one unified by the denial of conflict. Our very notion of the world – the capitalist twentieth century's 'one world' – is like a photographic overview. The world is 'one' not because it is united but because a tour of its diverse contents does not reveal conflict but only an even more astounding diversity. This spurious unity of the world is effected by translating its contents into images. Images are always compatible, or can be made compatible, even when the realities they depict are not. (*OP* 174)

This view of how the image world dissolves difference and conflict finds that the logic of capitalist society is fully compatible with that of photography: the 'logic of consumption' (*OP* 179). This argument is prefigured in an earlier essay when Sontag argues that people become ('through the camera') not only tourists but 'customers ... of reality', and the reality that is 'framed' and consumed is one that blurs any distinctions between originals and copies (*OP* 110). For Sontag, photography 'does not simply reproduce the real, it recycles it', and she finds this recycling well suited to a capitalist society's needs: 'The production of images also furnishes a ruling ideology … The freedom to consume a plurality of images and goods is equated with freedom itself' (*OP* 178-9).

On Photography evidences the hit and miss of speculative thinking as it moves between brilliant insight and banal generalisation. It offers an invigorating and contentious reading of aesthetic, moral, and political implications of photographic seeing. I want to critically examine some key assumptions underlying Sontag's many complaints 'against' photography and show that these complaints have their locus in specific *intellectual* anxieties. In *On Photography* Sontag returns once again to her long-standing interest in 'aesthetic ways of looking at the world', though on this occasion with a new and deeply pessimistic awareness of historical contexts.

It is possible to view the democratised vision of 'the image world' as a kind of perverse application of the pluralist claims for thought and culture Sontag advanced in the 1960s. Much of what she had to say on camp, for instance, could readily be applied to her reading of photographic seeing. The key common element is aesthetic detachment: 'Camp is the consistently aesthetic experience of the world', it is 'disengaged, depoliticised' and non-judgemental (*AI* 277). Sontag's claim in *On Photography* that photographs 'offer a connoisseur's relation to the world and a promiscuous acceptance of the world' (*OP* 79) formulates precisely the double nature of camp she identifies as its ability to simultaneously embrace and distance the world. Photographic seeing and camp taste are not one and the same thing. Sontag presents the former as a 'mass' phenomena not always conscious to the subject, the latter as 'a certain mode of aestheticism', a highly educated way of seeing which is self-conscious and intentionally parodic. Nevertheless, the connections are striking and suggest that she is once again deliberating on the interplay of elite and mass cultures. We recall that in 'Fascinating Fascism' she makes explicit her own elitism when she proposes 'the hard truth … that what may be acceptable in elite culture may not be acceptable in mass culture' (*USS* 98). The statement has a ring of resignation to it which chimes with her custodial relation to modernism in *Under the Sign of Saturn*. In *On Photography* this issue receives fuller treatment (though it is rarely so explicitly addressed) and is especially relevant to her claim that the aestheticism of photographic seeing is a generalised form of a once elitist taste. The elite taste and culture in question is Surrealism.

In the third essay of *On Photography*, 'Melancholy Objects', Sontag contends that photography 'is the one art that has managed to carry out the grandiose, century-old threats of a Surrealist takeover of the modern sensibility, while most of the pedigreed candidates have dropped out of the race' (*OP* 51). As in *Against Interpretation*, she is less interested in Surrealism as a particular artistic movement than as a sophisticated – ironic and promiscuous – aesthetic taste which is distinctively modern.[15] Her views on the relation of Surrealism to photography significantly influence her persistent focus on the discontinuity and disassociation of photographic seeing: 'Surrealism lies at the heart of the photographic enterprise: in the very creation of a duplicate world, of a reality in the second degree' (*OP* 52). Positing photography as *inherently* surreal, Sontag links the indiscriminatory nature of photographic seeing to the destructive career of modernity in its 'ceaseless replacement of the new' (*OP* 68) and consumerisation of the past. In *Against Interpretation* she had endorsed the witty Surrealist 'appreciation of the derelict, inane, *démodé* objects of Modern civilisation' (*AI* 271). In *On Photography* she questions the value(s) of Surrealism when 'we now make a history out of our detritus' (*OP* 68), not just an art. 'The Surrealist strategy', she writes, 'which promised a new and exciting vantage point for the radical criticism of modern culture, has devolved into an easy irony that democratises all evidence, that equates its scatter of evidence with history' (*OP* 75). The failure of the Surrealist strategy is the triumph of a generalised photographic seeing which accelerates a 'de-creation of the past' and 'invests the specificity of the past with an unlimited irony' (*OP* 77). When you accumulate fragments, Sontag implies, all you end up with is an accumulation of fragments.

In her commentary on Surrealism and elsewhere in *On Photography* Sontag is clearly examining her own aesthetic perspective and associations with 'radical' avant-gardism. Her approach to Surrealism is both more sceptical and more historical than in any of her previous writings (though there are echoes of her complaints with aestheticised radicalism in the late 1960s). She demystifies it as 'an aesthetic that yearns to be a politics' and describes it as a middle-class obsession, 'a bourgeois disaffection; that its militants thought it universal is only one of the signs that it is typically bourgeois' (*OP* 54). Sontag's critical commentary is generated, in part, by her sense of a new historical situation in which the 'logic of consumption' has rendered avant-garde strategies redundant. In a 1979 interview she is more explicit on this than she is in *On Photography*:

> There is really quite a close fit between avant-garde art and the values of the consumer society which needs products, constant turn-over, diversity, outrage and so on. The bohemian or radical artist's challenge of conventional bourgeois sensibility doesn't work any more. The consumer society is so sophisticated and so complex that it has broken down the lines between high and mass taste, between the conventional sensibility and the subversive sensibility.[16]

In the mid-1960s Sontag ironically observed that 'the history of the arts is a series of successful transgressions'. By the end of the 1970s she observes that transgression has become little more than an empty gesture: 'Transgression presupposes successful actions of order. But transgressions have become so successful that the idea of transgression has become normative for the arts.'[17]

Sontag is hardly sanguine about the 'success' of modernism, but there is a deeper political pessimism guiding her perspective in *On Photography*. This pessimism seems deliberately poised against the optimism (or more correctly what she reads as optimism) of Walter Benjamin about the political potentials of photography as a mechanically reproduced art form. In his famous 1936 essay on 'The Work of Art in the Age of Mechanical Reproduction', Benjamin argued that mechanical reproduction may promote a 'progressive reaction' within its mass audience, a reaction 'characterised by the direct, intimate fusion of visual and emotional enjoyment with the orientation of the expert'. For Benjamin, this progressive reaction encouraged 'critical collective abstractedness', a democratisation of political and critical possibilities. With reference to photography specifically he argued that the reproduction of prints exemplifies the erosion of 'authenticity' which transfers 'the total function of art' from the realm of ritual to that of politics.[18] It is precisely such a hope of political potential that much of *On Photography* would seem to question. While crediting Benjamin as 'photography's most original and important critic' (*OP* 76), Sontag implicitly questions the applicability of his views to a postindustrial consumer society. In such a society, she argues, 'our inclination is to attribute to real things the quality of an image' and photography exacerbates this inclination as it 'does not simply reproduce the real, it recycles it' (*OP* 174). For Benjamin, photographs can stimulate a 'dialectic of seeing' which illuminates the material history of cultural change and political struggle. For Sontag, the photographed image radically 'de-creates' the past, eroding historical connectedness or continuity. 'Through photographs', she writes, 'the world becomes a series of unrelated, freestanding particles' (*OP* 23).

Sontag's repeated emphasis on the atomised, dissociated experience of photographic seeing is such that she allows for no possibility that it promotes a 'progressive reaction'; it is, rather, fully habituated to the 'logic of consumption' which promotes an illusion of freedom and democracy while concealing a real lack of social or political change. (It is curious she does not acknowledge that Benjamin wrote insightfully and presciently about 'the illusion of democracy' he found implicated in the disjunction between the 'formal mobility' of social signs and 'a real mobility in social structures'.)[19] Sontag's thoroughgoing complaint against photography is also an indictment of the *pluralism* of the postindustrial consumer society which offers a franchised freedom of expression, innovation, and dissent. Her concerns about the equivalence of attention promoted by consumer pluralism are synonymous with her disquiet about the indiscriminatory way in which the democratic camera subsumes difference. The ways in which she conjoins these concerns is revealing of her own intellectual anxieties. Time and again in *On Photography* she denies photographs any cognitive or epistemic functions – 'The knowledge gained through still photographs will always be … a semblance of knowledge' (*OP* 24) – and insists that because photographs do not function in (narrative) time they 'cannot … explain anything' (*OP* 23). There is something narrow and overstated in this insistence, as she tends to focus on the photographed image as appearance rather than expression and does not allow for the possible continuity between the contexts in which photographs are produced and received.[20] This rigorous insistance that all photographic seeing is dissociated and lacking in cognitive assent promotes the moral alarm of *On Photography* and registers Sontag's distinct intellectual investment in the arguments she advances.

It is possible to view Sontag's anxiety about the dissociation of feeling and knowledge in capitalist society as a very old-fashioned one, but it has a fresh impetus (historical and personal) in her text, which underlines not only her critical investment in high modernism but also her left-liberal politics. In *On Photography* she formulates this anxiety from within and addresses it to a particular audience. It is in her lengthy critique of Diane Arbus that this is clearest. When she argues that: 'Arbus's work is a good instance of a leading tendency of high art in capitalist countries: to suppress, or at least reduce, moral and sensory queasiness', she also notes that such art is 'popular among sophisticated urban people right now: art that is a self-willed test of hardness' (*OP* 40). The theme of equivalence in photographic seeing which runs throughout *On Photography* takes on a particular political cast in Sontag's commentary on Arbus when she observes: 'Making equivalences between freaks, mad people, suburban couples, and nudists is a very powerful judgement, one in complicity with a recognisable political mood shared by many educated, left-liberal Americans' (*OP* 47). Sontag does little more to name this political mood, nor does she so directly address it or her readership at any other point in *On Photography*, but what she is diagnosing and warning her readers against is a false pluralism which feeds off a too complacent response to the democratised alienation of the 'image world'. Her left-liberal audience is subliminally encoded in keywords and phrases, as when she warns: '*Our ability* to stomach [a] rising grotesqueness in images … works out not as a *liberation* of but as a *subtraction from the self*' (*OP* 431, emphasis added); or again, in her rousing polemic against the politics of consumption in her final essay: 'The freedom to consume a *plurality* of images and goods is equated with *freedom itself*' (*OP* 178-9, emphasis added). Liberty, self, plurality, and freedom are watchwords of a liberal community. What *is* 'freedom itself'? Sontag assumes her readers know.

In her concern with liberal values Sontag echoes many other American intellectual voices of the mid-1970s. Much intellectual writing of the period is characterised by a sensed 'crisis of liberalism' and radical uncertainty about the parameters and functions of a public liberal culture. Such concerns are particularly clear in the work of intellectuals associated with New York – in the writings, for example, of Daniel Bell, Christopher Lasch, Harold Rosenberg, and Marshall Berman. Whatever their different positions along a liberal spectrum these intellectuals, like Sontag, are all agitated by their sense of forces ranged against the autonomy of self and of culture. To be sure, the differences are striking and important; Bell and Lasch, for instance, are scathing on the perversity of the 'subversive sensibility' as one of these forces, while Sontag sublimates this view to a more damning critique of the capitalist conditions which have neutered this sensibility by democratising it. Yet, these intellectuals share similar assumptions about the need for individual (especially ethical) responsibilities to a community. Lasch's pessimistic analysis of the 'narcissistic personality of our time' often echoes Sontag's views on 'chronic voyeurism', as when he observes that 'avoidance of emotional entanglements and of "judgemental" attitudes towards others reflects, at bottom, a narcissistic withdrawal of interest in the outside world. Other people matter only as they impinge on the self.'[21] Both intellectuals lament what Lasch terms 'the devaluation of values' and 'atomised individualism' in their culture.[22] In this they express not only a broadly liberal concern, but one that is much more narrowly intellectual.

Despite their different angles of approach to the ills of liberal culture, the intellectual values Sontag and Lasch share are evident in their intense concern for sceptical thought and rational discussion in the United States. For Lasch, the narcissistic sensibility corrupts 'prevailing modes of thinking and perception' producing 'intellectual apathy': 'The social order no longer excites a passionate curiosity to understand it.'[23] For Sontag, the image world defeats the very impetus to understand:

> Photography implies that we know about the world if we accept it as the camera records it. But this is the opposite of understanding, which starts from *not* accepting the world as it looks. All possibility of understanding is rooted in the ability to say no. (*OP* 23)

It is what she perceives as the image world's threat to this urge to understand that Sontag is most sensitive to, as a threat to her own intellectual legitimacy. Several reviewers of *On Photography* complained that Sontag heaped too many social ills on the medium. There is some truth in this, but I have preferred to ask why she should have done this. *On Photography* offers a displaced narrative of intellectual unease, a concern that the very conditions for critical intellectual thought (as she understands this) are diminishing in the United States. In a 1975 interview, conducted during the period she was writing her essays on photography, Sontag asserts: 'We live in a culture in which intelligence is denied relevance altogether … In my view the only intelligence worth defending is critical, dialectical, sceptical, desimplifying' (*SSR* 346). Where, in the early and mid-1960s, she could take these intellectual values for granted, and indeed draw on them to test the limits of a public liberal culture and of high modernist aesthetics, here, in the mid-1970s, she finds it necessary to defensively assert them.[24]

In Sontag's writings 'the ability to say no' is a correlative of her interest in the aesthetics of negation. By the late 1960s she was already aware that the spiritual rhetoric and critical power of modernism's negative dialectics were at a point of exhaustion. 'In my opinion', she writes in *Styles of Radical Will*, 'the myths of silence and emptiness are about as nourishing and viable as might be devised in an "unwholesome" time – which is, of necessity, a time in which "unwholesome" psychic states furnish the energies for most superior work in the arts. Yet one can't deny the pathos of these myths' (*SRW* 11). In the 1970s this sense of pathos overwhelms her interest in the contemporary arts, and in *Under the Sign of Saturn* she pays homage to the 'heroism' of selected modernists as against the grain of what she dismissively terms the 'facile eclecticism of contemporary taste' (*USS* 138). It is *On Photography* which explains her perception of this 'facile eclecticism', identifying it as the false intellectual economy and indiscriminatory pluralism of a consumerised modernism.

While Sontag's interpretation of the erosion of modernist tenets is clearly distinguished by her own intellectual values and assumptions it nonetheless shadows (and in many ways forecasts) key arguments of the emergent critical debate on postmodernism in the United States. In his seminal essay 'Postmodernism, or the Cultural Logic of Late Capitalism' (1984), Fredric Jameson posits postmodernism as a new 'cultural dominant', the term for 'a whole new culture of the image or the simulacrum' which has emerged in line with major changes in capitalist modes of production. In the contemporary stage of late capitalism, Jameson observes, 'aesthetic production ... has become integrated into commodity production generally'. The result is 'a transformation of the "real" into so many pseudo-events' and a concomitant erosion of 'depth models' of understanding (dialectical, Freudian, existential, and semiotic) and of 'the "semi-autonomy" of the cultural realm'. Detailing differences between modernism and postmodernism, Jameson very deliberately calls into question the ethos of negation commonly identified with the former and argues that the emergence of a postmodern aesthetic (characterised by 'a new kind of flatness and depthlessness') signifies an end to 'the great modernist thematics of alienation, anomie, solitude, and social fragmentation and isolation'.[25]

These are thematics of central importance in Sontag's writings and she is more reluctant than Jameson to pronounce them defunct, though by the mid-1970s she comes to believe they have been largely drained of their critical energies. While there is some common ground between her own and Jameson's perspectives she would baulk at his argument that conceptions of 'negativity, opposition, subversion … critique and reflexivity' are rendered redundant because they rely on a 'critical distance' which has been abolished by the conditions of postmodernity.[26] Sontag can only equate such a view with moral and political paralysis. In the face of her own pessimism she wants to hold on to her belief that it is possible to stand 'beyond culture', and much as *On Photography* is a study of the increased difficulties of doing this it is also – in its admixture of moral polemic and demystifying critique – an affirmation of her own critical distance. Her efforts to hold onto such a belief press her into close analysis of her tastes and values and impel her to test anew ideas of aesthetic comprehension against historical realities. The results reveal her own peculiar conflation of high modernism and left-liberalism around the ideal of critical negativity.

Given the development of Sontag's thinking about this ideal and her sense of its waning affect it is not surprising that melancholia comes to the fore in her 1970s writings both as a major theme and a sign of her critical temperament. While it is central to her study of the moderns in *Under the Sign of Saturn* a melancholy threnody also has a subdued presence in her writings on photography, which often seem haunted by an impossible desire for a more immediate, less 'image-choked world' (*OP* 15). In *On Photography*, though, she suggests that melancholia is deeply implicated in photography's 'de-creation' of the past, infecting vision with an immediate pathos and sentimentality (*OP* 71). Sontag is ambivalent about the seductiveness of melancholy perspectives. In her story 'Unguided Tour' (1978) this ambivalence is objectified in the predicament of the narrator, an unnamed 'woman of culture', who tells of her recent visit to a European city. The figures of the tourist, the flaneur, and the collector are combined in this narrator as she relates how she strolled the streets trying to differentiate between originals and copies, seeking the overlooked, 'the real thing' (*IE* 234). Her quest for the authentic is doomed to failure for the city is a museum-without-walls where the past is constantly on display and the authentic is coded and signposted as such.[27] Intensely self-conscious about her longings the narrator wants to deny her melancholy 'devotion to the past': 'I don't want to satisfy my desire', she tells her companion, 'I want to exasperate it. I want to resist the temptation of melancholy' (*IE* 240). For Sontag, the self-question-ing nature of the melancholy temperament offers some intellectual defence against the mindless accretions and fragmentations of history, knowledge, and subjectivity. It is, though, a defence (or defensiveness) that has its own pathos, for as Theodor Adorno once observed, 'subjective reflection, even if alerted to itself, has some-thing sentimental and anachronistic about it: something of a lament over the course of the world.'[28]

4

THE WAY WE LIVE NOW

In 1982 *A Susan Sontag Reader* was published, a collection of selected writings from *The Benefactor* through to her 1981 essay on Roland Barthes. Commenting on the reader in an interview Sontag describes it as marking the end of a distinct period in her writings: 'Now I feel I am at the beginning of another period ... I'm really a slow developer and my best is yet to come.'[1] If the *Reader* signified new beginnings, though, this looked for several years more like a loss of direction. With the signal exception of the essays in *AIDS and Its Metaphors* (1989), which advanced the analytical and diagnostic reasoning of *Illness as Metaphor* (1978) to the study of discourses surrounding AIDS, her essay writing was relatively low-key in this period. To be sure, essays continued to appear – on such diverse enthusiasms as Wagner, Robert Mapplethorpe, and seventeenth-century Dutch painting – but these are more isolated works than many of the essays that went before. Sontag's strong sense of her writings as a 'project', a self-absorbing cultural criticism which would define and clarify 'what it means to be modern', seemed to stall during a period when she had to reassess the relationship between her writing, her culture, and her audience.

Throughout the 1980s Sontag sought a wider distribution of her intellectual energies away from essay writing. In several interviews she said she saw her creative future in writing fiction and alluded to works-in-progress. Several short stories appeared, but it was not until 1992 that her third novel *The Volcano Lover* was published, twenty-five years after her second *Death Kit*. Drama also received a new interest as she directed plays by Kundera and Pirandello in the late 1980s. From the early 1980s onwards she stepped up her involvement in collective intellectual programmes and writers' gatherings, most of them based on international issues of human rights and freedom of expression. A founder-member of PEN American Centre, she became its president in 1986. As this range of activities would suggest, Sontag's intellectual vitality was not diminished in the 1980s. But there is also in this distended field of activities a perceptible effort being made by her to seek fresh channels for her generalism, while many of her writings show her disquiet about new difficulties in charting an independent intellectual path in her culture.

In the views of some commentators, Sontag began moving towards the political right in the 1980s. I argue this is a misreading of her intellectual trajectory which has too often been presented either as a judgement on her 'high' culture tastes or as a knee-jerk interpretation of her political statements in the context of a new 'cold war liberalism'. In some part it has been the very continuity of her cultural and political perspectives which has caused her to attract the conservative label. Many of her writings in the 1980s and since constitute a response to what she perceives as 'a widespread questioning ... of many of the ideals (and risks) of enlightened modernity' (AM 78-9). However ambivalently expressed (for she herself is involved in such questioning), her responses often transmit conservative overtones and appeals.

Starting from zero

If perceptions of Sontag's conservatism have been overstated this owes something to the major repatterning of intellectual politics in the United States in the 1980s. Among the cultural and political developments which had such a radical effect were the fragmentation and disorientation of the liberal left and the new public prominence of neoconservatism. These were not new developments and they have complex histories which constantly intersect, most notably in the late 1960s and early 1970s as the New Left fell apart as a coherent entity and neoconservatives (many of them from Old Left backgrounds) found a new force in attacking the perceived failings of the left and counter-culture. Throughout much of the 1970s intellectual politics in the United States had an appearance of windedness as an aftermath to the heightened radicalism of the 1960s, but in the late 1970s positions began to more visibly rigidify once again in a general climate of growing political conservatism. Throughout the 1970s Sontag tried to tack a course between political differences and antagonisms. While her left sympathies remained she also criticised what she saw as the anti-intellectualism of much left thinking.[2] Her broader political concern in this period was what she viewed as the decline of a public liberal sphere which would grant importance to the traditions of intellectual inquiry she had once taken for granted. With a new parochialism entering into left politics and the much publicised neoconservatism gathering momentum, any individual efforts to either transcend or steer a path between factions became more hazardous. Among New York intellectuals, with so many sensitive to the history of factional infighting, the politics of intellectual position-taking were felt and scrutinised especially keenly.

Sontag fell spectacularly foul of this new politicisation of intellectual differences in February 1982 following her speech at a public meeting in New York City's Town Hall. The meeting was organised to demonstrate support on the American left for the Polish Solidarity movement. Sontag chose this occasion to urge her left audience to 'rethink our position, and to abandon old and corrupt rhetoric', taking as her terms of reference not the immediate support for Solidarity but what she viewed as the American left's history of ambivalent and contradictory responses to communism. In a carefully worded speech, marked by aphoristic hyperbole and a tone of high reason, she informed her audience that 'the principal lesson to be learned' from the Polish events 'is the lesson of the failure of Communism, the utter villainy of the Communist system'. She charged that for fear of giving comfort to 'reactionary forces' people on the American left 'have willingly or unwittingly told a lot of lies' about communism when unequivocal criticism was needed. A confessional note is introduced as she recalls her own suspicions about the accounts of communism proffered by exiles from communist countries and discomfort with 'their truth', but she sees this as a collective failing of the left and 'I' becomes 'we' as she makes her judgements. Her speech contains blunt and harsh accusations that the American left not only found it difficult to formulate an adequate rhetoric of anti-communism, but failed to 'understand the nature of the Communist tyranny'. In explicating this failure Sontag outraged her audience. Among her most contentious statements, and certainly the most widely quoted, is the claim that the Polish events 'illustrate a truth that we should have understood a very long time ago: that Communism *is* fascism – successful fascism, if you will … Fascism with a human face'.[3]

Much of Sontag's speech was greeted by jeers and heckling. She later acknowledged that she had anticipated such an immediate reaction, but she was shocked by the scale and bitter virulence of the public responses which were to follow. The speech was widely picked up by newspapers and journals, with many replies appearing in New York journals for months afterwards. Several conservative commentators wrote happily of the speech as a renunciation of the American left. Most of the specially gathered responses were from the left and the great majority of these were highly critical of her comments. Some were annoyed at what they saw as the absolutism of her stance in refusing to discriminate amongst forms of communism. Others charged her with opportunism, political naïveté, and crudely resurrecting old arguments associated with 1950s anti-communism.[4] It is notable that many of the commentators on her speech viewed it as a recantation, a *mea culpa* which meant she was disavowing her leftist past and defecting to the opposition. Diana Trilling, for example, described the speech as 'an important defection from the ranks of intellectual sympathisers with Communism'.[5] Sontag's address was read in this way in part because it bore some of the generic hallmarks of 'the ex-sympathiser confessional'.[6] In 1982 this genre had a fresh resonance in a new cold war climate of ideological position-taking which saw many American liberals distinctly distancing themselves from the left.[7]

Sontag was angered by the reception of her speech as a recantation. Denying any 'defection to reaction' she patiently explained she had never been a communist 'and therefore am not now a "repentant" ex-Communist of the god-who-failed variety', and further explained that she had long been critical of communist regimes.[8] No matter, she was well and truly forked on an ideological dilemma she had hoped to transcend with her address. The irony was painful: having set out to open debate on the responsibilities of the left by exposing the ideological limitations of its rhetoric she found her own comments interpreted within the ideological cues of the 'old and corrupt' rhetoric of anti-communism she attacked. In a 1985 interview she ruefully reflects on the difficulties of transcending this dilemma: 'I'm not interested in giving aid and comfort to the neo-Conservatives. It's a crucifying dilemma … Since Town Hall it's been a disaster and I'm still digging my way out of the rubble.'[9] It is a little surprising she should have come so late to the realisation that her efforts to rationally mediate 'the relationship between intellectuals and the idea of revolution' would founder in ideological quicksand.[10] In her short story 'Old Complaints Revisited' (1975) the narrator, a member of an unnamed organisation, meditates on the difficulties of breaking ranks, wanting to declare 'What I believe is false' (*IE* 119) within the limits of ideological and rhetorical constraints without repudiating the 'sacrifice' of those in the organisation. The narrator hopes to transcend these constraints by setting out the 'illogic' of his/her position, yet is aware that members of the organisation will likely see this as repudiation 'and they would refuse to pardon me' (*IE* 103). The story seems prophetic in relation to her Town Hall address and its aftermath. Sontag spectacularly failed to transcend the ideological and discursive constraints she engaged – the result was her public burning.

Although widely read as a radical conversion narrative Sontag's Town Hall address is in many ways congruent with her intellectual style of rational clarification and demystification. It is not new for her to challenge what she views as debilitating choices between cultural or political positions. And when she describes her Town Hall address as 'my plea for intellectual honesty' this phrase finds echoes in much of her work as a valued rhetorical device. Similar calls to reason are issued in 'On Style', 'Trip to Hanoi', *On Photography*, *Illness as Metaphor*, and *AIDS and Its Metaphors*. In 'Old Complaints Revisited' the narrator trusts that the 'white magic of reason' (*IE* 129) will prove a liberation from perceived constraints. The ends may differ but the aim is general and constant in these calls to reason. To expose and transcend the constraints on thinking about a particular subject. At times in her work this aim has seemed more a haunting desire, as in 'Trip to Hanoi' when she muses on the obstacles of language and history which make it 'hard to step over one's own feet' (*SRW* 272). In 'Old Complaints Revisited' there is a deliberate intertextual allusion to this dilemma when the narrator recognises: 'My problem is identical with my language … If I could be silent, maybe I could walk over my own feet … But if I'm silent, how can I reason? And if I can't reason, how can I ever find a way out?' (*IE* 129-30). The language of reason is an alternative to silence in the powerplay of intellectual negations. We can see how such alternatives are sourced and proliferate in Sontag's work; they are at the very roots of her sense of intellectual being.

It is difficult to assess any lasting impact of the Town Hall imbroglio on Sontag's thinking or on her public image. Some have continued to view her as an eponymous 'Sixties' radical, and for her neoconservative critics this is a particularly useful association to keep alive as it serves to bracket and undermine her public voice. A notable example is Hilton Kramer who has penned several scathing attacks on her intellectual credibility. In an article entitled 'Anti-Communism and the Sontag Circle', published in *The New Criterion* in 1986, he depicts her at the centre of 'intellectuals who pride themselves on being culturally chic' and castigates her as an aesthete hopelessly ignorant of 'political realities'. For Kramer, 'neoconservatism … emerged from the turmoil of the Sixties to defend American democracy against the atrocious ideas of people like Susan Sontag'.[11] Kramer's comments are exemplary of the critical and often very public debate in the 1980s over the meaning and legacies of 'the Sixties'. Contrary to Kramer, though, the view that Sontag had disowned her Sixties past and moved to the right steadily gained public currency throughout the 1980s. (The Town Hall speech was certainly taken as some evidence of this but there are other markers as we shall see.) More and more in the 1980s she was cast by critics on the left as much as on the right as a 'celebrity intellectual', living off cultural capital accrued many years earlier and with little critical relevance to contemporary cultural politics.

What Sontag found slipping away from her in the 1980s was any strong sense of an intellectual community, either in the parochial sense of 'the New York intellectuals' or in the broader sense of 'educated, left-liberal Americans'. This was a community/audience she once took for granted. By the mid-1970s, as we have seen, she was already defensively asserting the need for a critical, sceptical intelligence as the *sine qua non* of this community. By the mid-1980s she is even more uncertain about her audience. 'I think', she comments in a 1985 interview,

> that there is generally less of a community and that the fragmentation of the left is a symptom. I think that it is less and less possible to take for granted certain cultural references. That's what a community is: taking for granted certain assumptions, not having to start from zero every time. This is no longer true.[12]

This lament was echoed by many among the older generations of left-liberal New York intellectuals. In the introduction to the fiftieth aniversary issue of *Partisan Review* in 1984 William Phillips spoke for many when he observed: 'Our literature, our culture, our politics are full of contradictions and reversals and polarisations.'[13] There were no great unifying issues and no singularised community of dissent. The liberal left was on the retreat, with many casting off their radical heritage or becoming nostalgic about it as a purer form of dissent in less complicated times.

The task of defining a public position and representing a broad constituency was more pressing for those New York intellectuals who were not neoconservatives. While neoconservatism is by no means a homogeneous intellectual movement its affiliates could speak with considerable confidence due to a surer sense of intellectual identity and purpose. A major 'strength of neoconservatism', Daniel Bell observed in 1984, is 'its critique of the simplicities of liberalism and of utopian illusions' (just such a critique is evidenced in Hilton Kramer's attack on Sontag).[14] And beyond such negative definitions of identity, the powerful emergence of conservative think-tanks meant real political influence. Moreover, at a time when it was widely proclaimed that the model of the free-wheeling, non-specialist intellectual was in terminal decline it was neoconservative writers who most visibly kept it alive. Intellectuals such as Irving Kristol, Norman Podhoretz, Hilton Kramer, Joseph Epstein, and many of their acolytes posed as the true heirs of the New York intellectual tradition, committed to 'the power of ideas' and writing in a public idiom for an educated middle-class audience.[15] However, their writings and political position-taking signified a self-conscious effort to strip this intellectual role of its associations with an ethic of dissent. Hand in hand with their attack on regnant left educators who politicise learning, neoconservative intellectuals sought to 'deradicalise' (Norman Podhoretz's term) the concept of intellect.

I neither want to overemphasise the power and prominence of the neoconservatives nor cast left-liberal intellectuals as a beleaguered minority. The latter did not go out of business in the 1980s, but they were often on the defensive, struggling to justify their politics and the contemporary relevance of their brand of cultural critique. For many New York intellectuals issues of intellectual legitimacy were further exacerbated by their distaste for the cultural politics of the academic left. Few on the academic left were trained in the New York style of public intellectual criticism or had much interest in the New Yorkers' political battles; indeed many were suspicious of the model of the public intellectual and distrusted the universalising language of left-liberal politics. While the New Yorkers bemoaned the new difficulties in defining unifying issues and assuming a 'common culture' many academics were keen to interpret positively the collapse of 'grand narratives' or unifying ideologies and were quick to point out that the concept of a common culture was a self-serving shibboleth of humanist intellectuals. The issues exciting many on the academic left were to be cast in a new critical style – with the rhetorics of radical theory privileging specialised and contingent forms of political thinking – one that was hostile to the archaic presumptions of the New York public intellectual.[16]

Sontag faced the same crises of legitimation and direction as many left-liberal intellectuals in the 1980s and had to make her choices of subject, argument, and audience with new considerations of her aims and public role. She had to find occasions to 'reason in public' under cultural and political conditions inimical to her belief in this as a necessary dissenting practice. While she volubly opposed neoconservatism she showed little interest in the main currents of the academic left's cultural politics. All too conscious of the rise of neoconservatism, she frequently argued it was more important than ever to defend the 'responsibilities' of intellectuals and reasserted her own sense of intellectual vocation. In a 1985 interview she comments:

> Currently intellectuals in Western Europe and North America are extremely demoralised and shaken by the rise of a virulent conservative tendency (which some have even joined). The way in which a certain kind of political idealism has been discredited and scorned makes the danger not that intellectuals keep on making fools of themselves, formulating political opinions when they might not be as informed as they might be, but that they retreat and leave politics to the professionals.[17]

Sontag is here promoting once again her belief in the value of intellectual 'amateurism' – the intellectual as non-specialist outsider who could bring an independent and fresh perspective – and moral consciousness-raising.

One of the arenas she found well suited to her own strong sense of 'political idealism' and the cry of moral outrage was the international forum or conference dealing with issues of human rights and freedom of expression. International writers' gatherings were not new, but in the 1980s they blossomed as never before and Sontag became a familiar participant.[18] PEN and other gatherings appear to have offered her a form of community and public platform suited to her intellectual vocation. This is not to question her commitment to any of her protest activities, but to suggest why this form should have been chosen. Within the 'international community' of writers there exists a common belief that the act of writing is a political (even a life and death) matter. Moreover, issues of human rights and freedom of expression may be treated in the language of universalist ideals, where the keywords are 'rights', 'humanity', 'morality', and 'conscience'. Per Wastberg, International President of PEN in the early 1980s, articulates the moral responsibility of writers:

> Writers, having no power, have moral authority ... The visions of our great poets and thinkers are not for escaping reality, not for easy solace, but for nourishment and energy, for forging new links, for inventing new solutions ... It is the never ceasing quest to expand the knowledge of mankind through imaginative work that International PEN defends by its charter.[19]

The writer holds a privileged position in the view of many PEN activists. In the words of Nadine Gordimer: 'If [the writer] is to work as well as he can, he must take and be granted, freedom from the public conformity of political interpretation, morals and tastes.'[20] Sontag could only agree with such views for they accord with her own long-held beliefs in the writer as a vanguardist voice of dissent and conscience.

The international writers' community and the politics of conscience have been important features of Sontag's public intellectual role in the last fifteen years. They have allowed her to keep alive in a very active way the ideas of autonomy and responsibility she associates with public thinking without leaving politics to the professionals (or to neoconservatives). However, when she has ventured towards the front lines of contemporary cultural politics in the United States – most notably with her essays on AIDS – her self-projection as a public intellectual presuming to address a general culture has met with considerable criticism.

Lethal metaphors

In the late 1980s Sontag found a subject which energised her critical thought, the subject of AIDS. In November 1986 her short story 'The Way We Live Now' appeared in the *New Yorker*. In 1989 she published the long essay *AIDS and Its Metaphors*. With AIDS Sontag had a subject about which she felt strongly and a subject which called on her modernist outlook as a defining issue, a locus of multiple cultural, social, and political representations and anxieties.

AIDS and Its Metaphors picks up and extends many of the concerns of *Illness as Metaphor*. Both texts have deeply personal origins. *Illness as Metaphor* was prompted by her own experience as a cancer patient and she wanted to illuminate and challenge the stigmatising functions of the cancer metaphor. 'My aim', she later observed, 'was to alleviate unnecessary suffering' (*AM* 13). In relation to her writings on AIDS she has said: 'It's impossible in New York not to know someone who's sick, or dying. In terms of trauma and grief it's the biggest event since the Vietnam War. It just goes on and on and on and you can't believe that it's not going to be over.'[21] In both texts she seeks to 'de-mythisize' (*IM* 11) disease; more pointedly she wants to elucidate particular metaphors in order to enact 'a liberation from them' (*IM* 7). This critical procedure and aim is what lends these essays their distinctive style and tone. For all the personal trauma and grief undergirding the essays the writing is patient and exacting, delineating and describing 'the uses of illness as a figure or metaphor' (*IM* 7). The writings appear austere and detached from their subject and what strikes the reader most powerfully is the process of a mind at work, steadily unpicking the meanings of metaphors in a manner which is remarkably fluid. The critical need to write on illness in a way that is 'useful' (*AM* 13) underlines Sontag's commitment to rationalising, descriptive critical prose and her belief in the power of intellect to challenge and reshape received forms of knowledge. The essays on illness are exemplary demonstrations of this belief.

Illness as Metaphor begins:

> Illness is the night-side of life, a more onerous citizenship. Everyone who is born holds dual citizenship, in the kingdom of the well and in the kingdom of the sick. Although we all prefer to use only the good passport, sooner or later each of us is obliged, at least for a spell, to identify ourselves as citizens of that other place. (*IM* 7)

That Sontag should choose to begin her essay with such a heavy dose of figurative language is clearly a deliberate ploy to underline the character and difficulty of her project, that of writing against metaphor itself. She goes on to make her point bluntly: 'My point is that illness is *not* a metaphor, and that the most truthful way of regarding illness – and the healthiest way of being ill – is one most purified of, most resistant to, metaphoric thinking' (*IM* 7). The call to resist metaphoric thinking is certainly not new in Sontag's writings, for it reprises her 'against interpretation' arguments. In a 1979 interview she comments on how metaphors can form a conceptual prison-house:

> Metaphors are central to thinking, but … you should know that they're a necessary fiction … it's a way of stopping your thinking and freezing you into certain attitudes. The intellectual project is inevitably involved with constructing new metaphors, because you have to use them to think, but at least you should be critical and sceptical of the ones you've inherited: unclogging your thought, letting in air, opening things out.[22]

This view of metaphor is reflected in the essays on illness, though with these essays Sontag lends this sceptical perspective a polemical thrust by arguing that disease should be literalised. When she asks her reader to 'regard cancer as if it were just a disease – a very serious one, but just a disease' (*AM* 14) she proposes that it is possible 'to deprive' (*AM* 14) an illness of its cultural nexus of meanings. In this vein her thinking is often strikingly platonic or empirical and at odds with a good deal of critical theorising on illness.

'Nothing', Sontag writes in *Illness as Metaphor*, 'is more punitive than to give a disease a meaning – that meaning being invariably a moralistic one' (*IM* 62). In this text she repeatedly targets for critical analysis the accusatory or stigmatising elements of selected metaphors. Her field is wide-ranging and marked by erudite referencing of diverse texts of classical, romantic, and modern literatures as well as medical theorising. There are, though, several key ideas carefully developed throughout the text which build outwards from her observations on moral and psychological judgements about the ill to implicate these judgements in broader cultural and political–economic anxieties. Metaphor naturalises, it bridges the known and the unknown, often to render the unknown understandable in conventional terms. In the case of disease this can work to determine and structure associated values and meanings in a manner which implies there is something singular about the people afflicted. In the case of diseases with no cure the propensity to metaphorise in a manner which is judgemental is most acute and the associations with otherness most alarming. *Illness as Metaphor* tracks the workings of these processes in responses to tuberculosis and cancer. Noting near the beginning of her study that TB and cancer share etymological origins Sontag goes on to outline different conceptions of the diseases and fantasies surrounding them, paying particular attention to how these fantasies are shaped by (and shape) 'modern' ideas of selfhood, civil (dis)order, and death. Taking as one major point of analysis 'the idea of the morbid' (IM 23) she examines how its meanings are patterned in diverse fantasies. The Romantics, she notes, not only moralised death in line with the etherialised personality of the TB patient, they used metaphors of the disease to 'aestheticise death' (IM 24). The beauty of the TB death resides in the association of the wasting body with heightened passion which is understood as the mark of a superior sensitivity, one transcendent of vulgar health. Sontag notes that in the early nineteenth century such a fantasy served class tastes and insecurities as the appearance of consumption could act as an index of gentility. In this development she identifies 'the first widespread example of that distinctively modern activity, promoting the self as an image' (IM 33). The romanticisation of TB contributed to the articulation of illness as *individual* – people are made singular by such a disease. The narcissism of this 'modern idea of individuality' has a significant aesthetic dimension – 'Sickness was a way of making people "interesting"' (IM 35) – and is strongly associated with ideas of intellectual refinement (dandyism) and extremity and with the melancholic temperament. Whatever her own identifications with such ideas (so strikingly confessed in the essays in *Under the Sign of Saturn*) Sontag chooses in this instance to coldly critique the aestheticisation of suffering as 'nihilistic and sentimental' (IM 36).

In moving from TB to cancer Sontag identifies how moralising judgements are attached to the disease through the process of metaphorisation and criticises conventional views on the existence of a personality type prone to contracting the disease. Cancer diagnosis, often seen as a sentence of death, generates a special kind of dread and she finds less evidence of cultural romanticisation in the metaphorisation of this disease. The move from TB to cancer is also one from romantic to modern in her text and she locates in theories about the emotional causes of cancer a heightened 'preoccupation with the isolated self' (IM 55) in the context of an over-productive capitalist consumer society. One of the most striking observations she makes about the metaphorisation of cancer is that it echoes and draws on particular discourses, most notably the language of capitalist expansion and the language of warfare. In economic terms cancer produces 'unregulated, abnormal, incoherent growth' (*IM* 67); it perverts and prevents (represses) the energy needed for indulgent consumption. The military language – cancer cells are 'invasive', they 'colonise' the body, overcoming its 'defenses' – is particularly significant in promoting conceptions of the disease as an 'enemy', a conception reinforced by governmental promises to 'wage war on cancer' (IM 70). With cancer so strongly identified as 'the disease of the Other' (*IM* 71) Sontag offers striking evidence for her argument that its metaphorisation exacerbates feelings of culpability in patients.

For Sontag, the metaphorisation of cancer acts as

> a vehicle for the large insufficiencies of this culture, for our shallow attitude toward death, for our anxieties about feeling, for our reckless improvident responses to our real 'problems of growth', for our inability to construct an advanced industrial society which properly regulates consumption, and for our justified fears of the increasingly violent course of history. (*IM* 89)

In short, the metaphorisation of cancer tells us much about 'what it means to be modern'. And in line with her consistent return to this metasubject she also returns to and extends established themes in her work: on the artist as exemplary sufferer, on melancholy, on 'the modern denial of death' (*IM* 12). Once again her writings are not only projected outwards to a 'general' culture, but inwards to the processes and enthusiasms of her own critical consciousness. While *Illness as Metaphor* rarely produces the epigrammatic density and flashing aphorisms of *On Photography* it is just as selective and partial in its treatment of ideas, and just as clearly works to display its incompleteness as symbolic of its provocative meditations. In *Illness as Metaphor*, as in *On Photography*, Sontag uses the essay form to clear space for critical thinking and in both texts her critical stance is most fundamentally an ethical one. (At the end of *Illness as Metaphor* she looks forward to a time when it 'will be morally possible, as it is not now, to use cancer as a metaphor' (*IM* 89).) The rigours of this stance predispose her to eschew autobiographical statement (she makes no reference to her own illness) while the idealism of such a stance leads her to polemicise 'against' metaphor. This approach appears quixotic in proposing a 'liberation' from metaphor, but underlying this polemical idealism is a strenuous moral effort to expose and resist the metaphorisation of illness as judgement.

This ethical stance is carried forward into *AIDS and Its Metaphors* where Sontag seeks to illuminate the moralising expolitation of AIDS. With this text the constraints she places on her act of interpretation make her approach seem wilfully blinkered, given the contexts of AIDS activism and the explosive cultural politics surrounding the disease. These contexts are barely acknowledged in her text. *AIDS and Its Metaphors* begins 'Rereading *Illness as Metaphor* now, I thought ...' (*AM* 5), and proceeds to explain why she wrote the earlier text. While such a beginning signifies her aim of extending her thinking on illness into a new context it is also an implicit assertion of her right to write on AIDS based on her intellectual authority and an indicator that the text we are about to read is a dispassionate meditation on its subject. Introducing the text in this way she seeks to transcend the politicised atmosphere surrounding AIDS.

Much of *AIDS and Its Metaphors* focuses on how the metaphorisation of AIDS has evoked and reinvented the idea of disease as judgement. AIDS, Sontag declares, has usurped cancer as 'the generic rebuke to life and to hope' (*AM* 24) and she contrasts the processes of stigmatisation associated with each. Where cancer is often linked to 'a weakness of the will or lack of prudence' AIDS is associated with 'indulgence, delinquency – addictions to chemicals that are illegal and to sex regarded as deviant' (*AM* 25). Where cancer may cause patients to experience shame and wonder why they contracted the disease, with AIDS 'the scandal is not at all obscure' for 'to get AIDS is precisely to be revealed, in the majority of cases so far, as a member of a certain "risk group", a community of pariahs' (*AM* 24-5). Such constructions of identity, in Sontag's view, mark a shift in the moralising of disease. Where the metaphorisation of cancer as a judgement on the individual reflects modern secular ideas of selfhood, AIDS, she argues, is widely interpreted in pre-modern terms as a 'collective judgement' on particular communities and even whole societies.

It is this conception of AIDS as collective judgement which is facilitated by its metaphorisation as a plague and Sontag comments insightfully on the historical development of the plague metaphor and its contemporary usage. Noting that the metaphor is usually applied to epidemics she argues that this application is distinctly selective, it is 'the most feared diseases, those that are not simply fatal but transform the body into something alienating' (*AM* 45) – leprosy, syphilis, and cholera, say, but not influenza or polio. The metaphorisation of AIDS follows what she terms the 'classic script for plague' (*AM* 51) in the inflation and manipulation of cultural fears and anxieties. One example is the common conception of inexorability, associated with its viral character, which imputes a particular terror to AIDS. The virus is terrifying not because it 'invades' the body but because it is latent and infectious; it is associated with mutation and contamination in ways that are characterised as 'implacable' and 'insidious'. The viral imagery promotes the common sense of AIDS as omnipresent and 'an entirely new disease – a new judgement' (*AM* 71). Another example of the use of the plague metaphor, echoing long-established links 'between imagining disease and imagining foreignness' (*AM* 48), is the view of AIDS as 'another infestation from the so-called Third World' (*AM* 52). If AIDS were confined to Africa, Sontag suggests, it would be seen as a 'natural disaster' but because it affects the West 'it is filled with historical meaning' (*AM* 83). At the same time the plague metaphor can be cast as a judgement on forms of otherness within Western social orders, serving 'First World political paranoia' (*AM* 62) and the manipulation of 'consensus-building fears' (*AM* 63). Sontag notes the 'utility of AIDS' for neoconservatives wanting to inflate complaints about permissiveness and further 'the Kulturkampf against all that is called, for short (and inaccurately), the 1960s' (*AM* 63).

While drawing attention to many ways in which metaphors shape private perceptions and provide insidious rhetorical support for public policies, Sontag cannot resist the symbolic sweep of viewing AIDS as a *fin de siècle* crisis. 'The catastrophe of AIDS', she writes,

> suggests the immediate necessity of limitation, of constraint for the body and for consciousness ... There is a broad tendency in our culture, an end-of-an-era feeling, that AIDS is reinforcing; an exhaustion, for many, of purely secular ideals – ideals that seemed to encourage libertinism or at least not provide any coherent inhibition against it – in which the response to AIDS finds its place ... The response to AIDS, while in part perfectly rational, amplifies a widespread questioning that had been rising in intensity throughout the 1970s of many of the ideals (and risks) of enlightened modernity.
>
> (*AM* 78-9)

These comments indicate Sontag's more 'general' intellectual concerns in writing about AIDS. Throughout her writings she has contended with the cultural meanings of the exhaustion of 'enlightened modernity', and it is not new for her to point up 'an end-of-an-era feeling' as so much of her work posits a sense of an ending that colours the most diverse cultural events and practices. With reference to AIDS she sees an intensification, even absoluteness, in such thinking for it marks a new attitude towards catastrophe. The apocalyptic rhetoric surrounding AIDS, she argues, connotes not only a need to control fear but 'also expresses an imaginative complicity with disaster' (*AM* 86), making of AIDS 'a catastrophe in slow motion' (*AM* 88) which shadows the (post)modern imagination of a dystopian future while numbing us to present realities.

While *Illness as Metaphor* was widely lauded as a critical *tour de force*, *AIDS and Its Metaphors* met with more mixed reviews, many of them hostile. Michael Ignatieff saw in both texts 'an exemplary demonstration of the power of intellect in the face of the lethal metaphors of fear'.[23] But for many Sontag's intellect is too prominent, her stance too detached from her subject. Richard Goldstein faults her silence on AIDS 'realities': 'Sontag's perch on the epidemic requires that she distance herself from its grimy, seamy realities. She is quite willing to reach for the stars when it comes to cultural synthesis, but oddly remote when it comes to the battle over condoms and clean needles.'[24] Several reviewers questioned her usage of specific words and phrasing in describing gay sexuality to argue that her point of view is not clear in her text and even implicitly judgemental of gay sexual practices. D. A. Miller charges that her language is disingenuous in that it works to deny, 'in the form of an invitation to move beyond, the specifically gay bearing of AIDS metaphors'.[25] Miller has been one of Sontag's most damning critics, arguing that her intellectual 'urbanity' is complicit with homophobia and cultural conservatism; in a lengthy close reading of *AIDS and Its Metaphors* he seeks out its political unconscious to claim that the text stands 'in the same irrationally phobic relation to AIDS that [Sontag] alleges an interest in demystifying'.[26]

If Sontag hoped to 'calm the imagination, not to incite it' (*AM* 14) this met with limited sympathy from reviewers or respondents. Her intellectual 'urbanity' was a problem for many critics, at the very least as evidence of a mandarin insensitivity if not (as Miller argues) a covert neoconservative agenda. In her efforts to 'de-dramatise' disease Sontag hoped to clarify and transcend the interpellating and more particularly stigmatising uses of metaphor. This is not only a self-styled ethical project but a vigorously rationalist one. Near the end of *AIDS and Its Metaphors* she avers that the process of stigmatisation 'is always worth challenging' and speculates that this process

> does seem to have more limited credibility in the modern world, among people willing to be modern – the process is under surveillance now. With this illness, one that elicits so much guilt and shame, the effort to detach it from these meanings, these metaphors, seems particularly liberating, even consoling. But the metaphors cannot be distanced just by abstaining from them. They have to be exposed, criticised, belaboured, used up. (*AM* 94)

Sontag's rationalist stance is uncompromising: it is the condition of 'people willing to be modern' and the mirror of her intellectual self-conception. It is a stance which can provoke opposition when she chooses to 'reason in public'. With *AIDS and Its Metaphors* (as with her infamous Town Hall speech) many among her 'audience' have proved unwilling to accept her corrective intellectualising.

To recognise Sontag's commitment to intellectual reasoning and concerns about the collapse of the project of enlightened modernity should not necessarily mean equating her stance and rhetoric with neoconservative perspectives. Nor does the impersonality of her writing necessarily disqualify her sense of moral outrage. Wayne Koestenbaum recognises that her 'first wish is to project ... an aura of measured inquiry, of reason's sway' and notes that many readers still 'want to think that critical omniscience is still feasible'. While critical of her silence about the politics of AIDS activism he further observes that she 'speaks to a broader public' (than the activist or academic) who may not celebrate gay sexual feelings and that her central arguments about the metaphorisation of AIDS are *not* universally accepted and need the publicity of her writing. Where Miller sees a phobic response to AIDS in the conscious artifice of Sontag's essay writing Koestenbaum sees a defensive yet deeply personal intellectual act: 'Any occasion in which *writing* asserts itself as an intransitive process bears a moral stamp; watching a writer in motion, we are encouraged to see text as a model of other drives, other exercises. Because of its self-consciousness, [Sontag's] essay is intimate; it is more than, and less than, social commentary.'[27]

Sontag's 'against interpretation' strategy in *AIDS and Its Metaphors* obscures as much as it exemplifies her own anxieties about intellectually controlling metaphors of fear. It is not surprising if readers take her silences to mean disinterest in the urgency of the epidemic. It may be that her short story 'The Way We Live

Now' is more successful in giving powerful and poignant expression to 'the universe of fear in which everyone now lives' (*AM* 73). The story consists of conversations surrounding a man dying from AIDS and explores the micropolitics of the relationships between the dying man and his friends and lovers. As the voices are carefully orchestrated around the silent centre (the dying man does not speak) the various emotional tones and moods take on a compelling force, convincing the reader that this is indeed a 'catastrophe in slow motion'. The story bares its artifice to suggest that language is used in an effort to control the disease and that narrative, through indirection and deferral, acts as a stay against death. The search for meaning is moving and pathetic; everyone is eager to say and to be heard to say the right thing, but their efforts topple toward banality ('when something like this happens (the sky is falling, the sky is falling!) you understand what's really important'). 'Fear gives everything its hue, its high', the patient is reported to have said, and fear ripples through the conversations surrounding him. And yet this is not a story of certain death and isolation, for Sontag stresses the strength of community and offers hope of transcending horror and grief.[28] 'The Way We Live Now' is a daring application of the aesthetic of silence which renders the reality of AIDS more immediately personal than *AIDS and Its Metaphors*.

As 'The Way We Live Now' indicates, Sontag is as much interested in the private truths as the public lies surrounding AIDS. To be sure, her generalist concern with the imagination of disaster AIDS embodies and emboldens can seem dilettantish when set beside the texts and politics of activism initiated by diverse individuals and groups in the United States and beyond. But while her own imagination of disaster abstracts, silences, and generalises, it also sharpens her sense of a need to oppose the 'violence that is being done to our sense of reality, to our humanity' (*AM* 93) by metaphors of fear. Her effort to think 'against' metaphor is, of course, an act (and affirmation) of critical negation. If this is a self-consciously quixotic act in her writings on illness it is also a moral plea to resist the imminence of crisis the most punitive and despairing metaphors reinforce. *Illness and Metaphor, AIDS and Its Metaphors*, and 'The Way We Live Now' are among her most personal and impassioned writings, fiercely critical of moralising distinctions between the sick and the well. What these texts tell us about 'the way we live now' is that we have all become victims of representations of disease and are the more poorly prepared for the 'onerous citizenship' of illness.

The world upside down

Throughout the 1980s Sontag's interest in the essay form diminished. She has said she came to find it a restricting form, only allowing her to express her feelings indirectly; 'very slowly', she remarks in a 1992 interview, 'I've been trying to choke off the essayistic voice'.[29] She began to feel the novel form offered her a way to explore the pleasures of narrative so rigorously controlled by her essayistic voice. The experience of writing *The Volcano Lover*, which she began at the end of the 1980s and published in 1992, seems to have been cathartic for her. Her excitement is palpable in several interviews as she relates the sense of discovery in writing the novel: 'It's only in the writing of this book that I discovered that I could narrate', she tells one interviewer, 'The whole novel was a discovery of furious permissions I granted myself.'[30]

At first sight the novel seems an astonishing departure from anything she had written. *The Volcano Lover* is a historical romance, its subject is the infamous love triangle between Sir William Hamilton, Emma Hamilton, and Horatio Nelson, and its central setting is late-eighteenth-century Naples where Hamilton was the British envoy to the court of the Bourbon rulers. This is hardly the genre or the subject matter readily associated with Sontag. On closer inspection, though, we find she has not sold out her intellectual credentials but has turned in something of a 'postmodern potboiler', a metafictional treatment of a much told story and highly conventionalised genre. *The Volcano Lover* is not a cold intellectual labour of postmodern tricksiness, for Sontag seems to have been genuinely enthralled by the world of her narrative and keen to engage the reader in the passions she describes – turbulent passions surrounding art, love, and revolution. But she is rarely able to let go of her critical consciousness and have her characters show us these passions, rather she describes them and constantly reminds her reader of her and our distance from the world of the text. The Hamiltons and Nelson are not mentioned by name in the novel, rather Sontag employs a theatrical device of labelling them 'the Cavaliere', 'the Cavaliere's wife' and 'the hero'; they are stage figures, or mythical figures, playing out roles she assumes her readers are familiar with. Along with this stylisation there are numerous contemporary references in the novel and an ironic contemporary voice commenting on the melodramatic proceedings.

The contemporary perspective and tone in themselves could be

irritating if not aligned with the novel's themes, but these are generally well aligned. Sontag wants to reinforce our perception of the
relationship between then and now: the historical eruptions of late-
eighteenth-century Europe are echoed in the late-twentieth-
century European present, it is the end of an old order and the
beginning of the new. At one point the narrator observes 'to live
among ruins – Naples, or Berlin today – is to be reassured that one
can survive any disaster, even the greatest' (VL 162) – Sontag lived
in Berlin while writing The Volcano Lover. But there are no tightly
drawn analogies between the past and present periods of revolution,
for she is less interested in the specifics of political revolution than
in the climate – emotional and intellectual – of radical change. The
civil disorders and political revolutions of the late eighteenth century
are significant to her as markers of a broader experience of change,
'the beginning of the time we call modern' (VL 115). It is the beginning of the time when (in Marx's phrasing) 'all that is solid melts
into air' as established roles and values come into crisis. The Volcano
Lover portrays the explosive dialectics of ethics and aesthetics,
reason and religion, democracy and monarchy. At the centre of it all
is the volcano, Mount Vesuvius, an over-determined metaphor –
'violent convulsion, upheaval from below, and waves of lethal force
that harrow and permanently alter the landscape' (VL 161) – for all
the varieties of passion on display.

The 'volcano lover' of the title is Sir William Hamilton, the
Cavaliere, and it is his experiences and perspectives which receive
the greatest degree of attention in the narrative. Though in historical legend he is little more than a famous cuckold, for Sontag he is a
character of considerably more interest, a man who 'thought of
himself as – no, was – an envoy of decorum and reason' (VL 56) in a
world of uncontrolled passions. He is a 'fastidious spectator' (VL
135) of the events around him and in Naples he responds to 'life as
a spectacle'(VL 21):

> He is interested in everything. And he lives in a place that for
> sheer volume of curiosities – historical, natural, social – could
> hardly be surpassed … On the streets life piled up, extruded,
> overflowed. Certain court celebrations included the building
> in front of the royal palace of an artificial mountain festooned
> with meat, game, cakes, and fruit, whose dismantling by the
> ravenous mob, unleashed by a salvo of canon, was applauded
> by the overfed from balconies … Where those stunned by the
> horror of the famine and the brutality and incompetence of

the government's response saw unending inertia, lethargy, a hardened lava of ignorance, the Cavaliere saw a flow ... The Cavaliere had never been as active, as stimulated, as alive mentally. As pleasurably detached.   (*VL* 20-2)

Hamilton has a distinctively aesthetic taste for disaster. A renowned collector and 'connoisseur of ruins' (*VL* 57) he is also a creature of melancholy whose 'astonishing spread of enthusiasms' (*VL* 20) act as a goad to activity and a stay against the irrationalities which threaten his composed detachment.

In the figure of Hamilton Sontag combines a range of characteristics and perspectives common in her writings, those of the aesthete, the melancholic, the tourist, the connoisseur of ruins, the collector. In 'Under the Sign of Saturn' she comments on how modernism reinvents 'the baroque cult of ruins; to perceive that the nihilistic energies of the modern era make everything a ruin or fragment – and therefore collectible' (*USS* 120) In many of her writings she further explores this allegorical and aesthetic idea of the modern. In *On Photography*, for example, she contends that photography 'extends the eighteenth-century literati's discovery of the beauty of ruins into a genuinely popular taste' (*OP* 79) and so 'photographic seeing' instantly 'beautifies' and 'antiques' reality. With *The Volcano Lover* she explores historical roots of the 'aesthetic sensibility' she has long been both fascinated and appalled by.

Hamilton prizes his melancholy detachment, wanting to refine it and objectify it as the emblem of his identity. This he does through his self-identification as a collector who feeds his egotism by heroic self-effacement before 'beautiful things'. A diplomat expert in the political arts of dissimulation, Hamilton is also a closet misanthrope resistant to change and deep emotional feelings. Collecting – the world of things – offers him a form of ontological security, a means of viewing the world with equanimity and engaging its violence vicariously. 'It is my nature to collect', he states, and the narrator explains: 'Collecting expresses a free-floating desire that attaches and re-attaches itself – it is a succession of desires. The true collector is in the grip not of what is collected but of collecting' (*VL* 24). What seems natural is artificially cultivated, as Hamilton seeks to achieve a life of perfect decorum or 'felicity' (*VL* 340) in his succession of desires. Ultimately, he desires for himself the aesthetic autonomy he admires in art and in his beautiful objects. Collecting projects an ideal of self-sufficiency and so he gives his life to the cultivation of an obsessive sensibility.

Sontag is once again exploring the 'aesthetics of silence' in the absoluteness of Hamilton's obsessions. The collector, the narrator comments, is 'motivated by the desire for completeness', while this is understood not as a quest for a complete collection (the metonymy of desires being interminable) but as a sensual and imaginative need 'for excess, for surfeit, for profusion' (*VL* 72). Implicit in this need is 'the collector's fantasy of ideal self-sufficiency' (*VL* 340). For Hamilton this fantasy is most powerfully imaged in his fascination with Mount Vesuvius. He studies, climbs, and watches the volcano, taking pleasure in its dangerous instability. His narcissism and sense of spectacle combine to make the volcano 'a stimulus for contemplation' (*VL* 82). The observatory which he has built on his Naples mansion is a circular room, one half taken up by a balconied window, the other by mirrored walls, and so allows him to multiply 'the view he commands – installed in the middle of it, as on a cliff. Or in a camera obscura' (*VL* 74). This is the very image of his idealised aesthetic state, for he is both subject and object of his gaze, a figure in a landscape utterly contained within his own vision.

As Naples, 'so rewardingly isolated from transforming events … [is] dragged into what passed then for the real world, the one defined by the threat of France' (*VL* 134-5), Hamilton's world is turned upside down. The carnivalesque spectacle of Naples gives way to revolutionary terror and violence and Hamilton proves to be a connoisseur of disaster who is 'ill-prepared … for the real thing' (*VL* 145). His sense of 'complicity with destructiveness' (*VL* 82) had always required an aesthetic framework, an appropriate perspective upon and distance from the real. He is now confronted with a world wherein neither his knowledge nor his passions confirm his identity. Hamilton is unable to recognise his 'complicity' in the horrifying human violence which erupts in Naples during the Jacobin insurrection, nor in that engineered by Nelson who later executes hundreds of the revolutionaries. Once proudly detached he becomes simply passive, telling himself (as his old friends are executed): 'Be calm. You cannot help. It is out of your hands' (*VL* 297), and accepting Nelson's rationalisations, 'we cannot interfere with the course of justice … for the sake of the civilised world.' (*VL* 298-90). But his complicity is nonetheless apparent to the reader, for we are asked to recognise that his investment in the old order is identical with his passions and perspectives as a collector. His socio-political perspectives are congruent with his aesthetic passions, for he wants a perfect (rational) equilibrium of passions to be reflected in the world around him, a hierarchy of social order in which thought governs action and the individual governs the mass. Hamilton's prized detachment is also revealed as an ideological component of a wider imperialism – notably, many of his most precious artefacts are stolen from Roman ruins – his desire to conserve conceals a history of violent destruction.

Sontag's own modernist perspectives and passions are under scrutiny in *The Volcano Lover*, and the novel provides a fascinating tableau of conflicting ideas about aesthetic and political imperatives. There is much the author can identify with in the figure of Hamilton, but it is at best an ambivalent identification for the narrative sharply critiques his moral equivocations and self-serving politics while positing these as inseparable from his refined aesthetic temperament. As we have seen, Sontag has long held a strong identification with the aesthetic connoisseurship and melancholia of modernist thinking. In certain writings these interests are isolated and projected onto selected individuals (Walter Benjamin as melancholy collector, or Roland Barthes as aesthete), in others they are historicised and critically demystified (as with her analyses of the middle-class roots of modern aestheticism in *On Photography* and *Illness as Metaphor*). In *The Volcano Lover* these interests are more radically reshuffled and dealt to us as a melodrama of passions. While Sontag clearly wants us to believe in her novel as a historical melodrama it also functions as a dramaturgy of ideas and, more obliquely, as an allegorisation of conflicts in her self-identification as a modernist intellectual.

Perhaps the most revealing (and somewhat surprising) element of this self-questioning in the novel is the attention Sontag gives to distinctively female experiences and perspectives. Her claim that *The Volcano Lover* 'speaks in many voices' is a little misleading as Hamilton clearly dominates the narrative, but there are other voices and the ones which most compellingly pull our attention away from Hamilton are those of women. Although all the characters are role-playing in this historical melodrama the performance of identity is the more acutely experienced and politically charged for women in the male dominated world of the text. As the narrator observes, 'Women are trained to be marginal or supporting players in that world ... To compete for approbation – not to compete as such' (*VL* 138).

Emma Hamilton embodies, in a suitably exaggerated form, key motivations and functions of a theatrical femininity. Hamilton

receives Emma as his nephew's discarded mistress and his relationship to her develops as that of a collector to a work of art. He sees in
Emma 'the beauty he had adored on canvas, as a statue, on the side
of a vase' (*VL* 130). Unlike Hamilton, Emma has little capacity for
irony or melancholy detachment, she is cheerfully vulgar and her
beauty is described as that 'of someone who has to fight for a place
and can take nothing for granted. Beauty which is about volume,
which is willing to be, cannot choose to be other than, flesh' (*VL*
132). While admiring this beauty Hamilton also wants to put it on
display and have it recognised as 'the proud possession … of a great
collector' (*VL* 132). The most dramatic display he devises is a *tableau
vivant* of classical scenes which involves Emma 'in a sequence of
poses, a living slide show of the iconic moments of ancient myth and
literature' (*VL* 146). As her poses rapidly change in performance,
the narrator comments:

> Change without transition. From sorrow to joy, from joy to
> terror. From suffering to bliss, from bliss to horror. It seems
> the ultimate feminine gift, to be able to pass effortlessly, in-
> stantly, from one emotion to another. How men wanted
> women to be, and what they scorned in women. One minute
> this. The next minute that. (*VL* 147)

For much of the narrative it seems that these simulations of femininity mirror and supplement Emma's social 'role as [Hamilton's]
companion, as a lady in training' (*VL* 163). But Emma is also an
'independent woman surviving … by her wits and talents' and a
woman with a strong desire to be seen 'as herself, no longer a model
but a subject' (*VL* 177). As the narrative develops she does become
more fully a subject; though in her actions she continues to seek
approbation from men, she more assertively selects and performs
the roles she wants. In the public drama of her relationship with
Nelson her display of autonomy is widely demonised in gossip and
caricature as that of 'a woman exercising inappropriate power' (*VL*
299). Emma's most directly voiced feelings are given to us post-
humously near the end of the text. Reflecting on her final years
lived in poverty she sees herself as 'a tragic figure' (*VL* 403) and has
few regrets: 'My life had great velocity. Then it was spent' (*VL* 407).

Emma's reflections constitute one of four lengthy monologues
which close the novel. All four are posthumous, in the style of an
operatic epilogue, and all are voiced by women – Catherine (Hamilton's first wife), Mrs Cadogan (Emma's mother), Emma, and the

poet Eleonora Fonseca di Pimental. Of these it is Fonseca who provides the most dramatic and damning judgements on the characters and events of the narrative – and who seems most closely identified with Sontag herself. Fonseca, a noblewoman who gave herself over to the cause of revolution, voices a passionate condemnation of the wealthy and refined few who ruled her world. Aware that she talks 'like a woman of my class' she is also self-critical about her failures to identify herself politically as a woman as well as a revolutionary. Her monologue ends:

> For all my certitude, I feared I would never be strong enough to understand what would allow me to protect myself. Sometimes I had to forget that I was a woman to accomplish the best of which I was capable. Or I would lie to myself about how complicated it is to be a woman. Thus do all women, including the author of this book. But I cannot forgive those who did not care about more than their own glory or well-being. They thought they were civilised. They were despicable. Damn them all. (VL 419)

Fonseca may be intended as a deliberate contrast to Emma, a highly educated woman who 'did not drown in the love of a single person' (VL 413) but rather committed her passions to literary and political realms. Even without the authorial self-reference in these lines it would be difficult not to see Fonseca as her author's double: a writer and activist who has disavowed aspects of her identity as a woman because she moved (intellectually) in a world of men and wanted to succeed on established terms.

As these are the closing lines of The Volcano Lover it is tempting to ascribe considerable weight to them – the author's judgement or self-revelation? Some reviewers have felt that the condemnation of the central characters by Fonseca is too little too late in a narrative mostly given over to these characters. Some have interpreted these lines as a vain apologia, or as an unconvincing rush of 'pious feminist sentiments'.[31] These lines should not be too hastily read as the author's summary statement on her central characters or on her intellectual career. I have no doubt Sontag means to acknowledge a conflict between her commitment to feminism and her desire to live (and write) up to an ideal of intellectual independence, but in this novel as in so many of her writings it is (to paraphrase Sontag on Walter Benjamin) important to her to keep her many 'positions' open (USS 133). To view The Volcano Lover as a dramaturgy of ideas is to recognise that 'Sontag' is not simply to be identified with any one character, for her identifications or self-projections are split between several. I would argue she identifies as strongly with Hamilton's connoisseurship and melancholy detachment as she does with Fonseca's political zeal and intellectual ardency; she has also expressed her admiration of Emma Hamilton's capacity for self-invention.[32] The characters embody specific temperaments or ideas which are difficult to reconcile – rational order and romantic excess, melancholia and exuberance, conservation and destruction – and which are recognisably the product of the author's intellectual passionaria.

I do not mean to suggest that there is a perfect equilibrium of conflicting ideas in the novel, nor that Sontag lacks any serious commitment to those advanced (including Fonseca's feminist horizon). There is clearly an intent to move the narrative through a range of specific temperaments in a manner which undermines Hamilton's assumptions about the sufficiency of melancholy detachment. This movement in itself would seem to have a personal import for Sontag. In a 1993 interview she suggests that with *The Volcano Lover* she might 'have finally transcended my own fixation on [melancholy]'.[33] Considering this movement, the ending of the novel might be read as a critical perspective on the more conventionally male authorisation and authority of the modernist ideals Sontag has long identified with. However, even if such a critique is her intent (and notwithstanding her exuberance about having written a novel which allows her to overcome the impersonality of the 'essayistic voice'), *The Volcano Lover* remains a deeply modernist text. If Hamilton's volcano represents his narcissistic and conservative desires it might also stand as a figure of the modernist 'magic mountain', an autonomous site of rarefied intellectual pleasures and ascetic contemplation. Whatever Sontag's desire to critique the presumptions of such an imaginative autonomy it is still the position she assumes in writing. In her memoir 'Pilgrimage', we recall, she comments on her early fascination with Thomas Mann's *The Magic Mountain*: 'There on the mountain, characters were ideas and ideas were passions, exactly as I'd always felt' – and exactly as they are depicted in *The Volcano Lover*.

Conclusion

THE LAST INTELLECTUAL

Reviewing *The Volcano Lover* John Banville wondered if 'even the profoundest critics are not content merely to criticise fiction, but itch also to produce the stuff'.[1] Following publication of the novel Sontag told several interviewers it represented a turning point in her career and the fulfilment of a long-held desire to launch herself fully as a novelist. 'This book is the best book I've ever written,' she tells one interviewer, 'I don't want readers to take my books off their shelves but I feel like I'm beginning again ... I'm a slow developer. I may have seemed precocious but it's taken me almost thirty years to get up the nerve to do what I think I can do.'[2] This is the enthusiasm of a born again novelist who believes she has overcome the impersonality of her prose style and found a more direct way of expressing her 'passions'.[3] While it is clear the essay form no longer satisfies Sontag's aims and ambitions as a writer it is too early to say if her turn to the novel signifies any major change in her critical and cultural perspectives or if it will constrain her generalist instincts. Although she is contracted to publish four novels she is unlikely to confine herself to fiction. Her most recent publication is her first play *Alice in Bed*.[4]

We should recognise that Sontag's rhetoric of new beginnings is not new, for she has said at several points in her career that she is starting over and has always portrayed herself 'in flight from [her] past work'.[5] Her 'working illusion' of being self-created generates this flight as she constantly revises her 'positions' and makes a dramaturgy of her ideas and passions. What she says of Roland Barthes's 'multiple identifications' is true of her own:

Barthes's work – he avows that he writes by obsessions – consists of continuities and detours; the accumulation of points of view; finally, their disburdenment: a mixture of progress and caprice … The writer's freedom that Barthes describes is, in part, flight. The writer is the deputy of his own ego – of that self in perpetual flight before what is fixed by writing, as the mind is in perpetual flight from doctrine. (*SSR* 443)

Sontag's writing is similarly self-cancelling, seeking out opposing positions so as to test her critical assumptions. Ambivalence is the reigning modality of feeling in her work, most obviously in the essays where she writes an antithetical criticism, formally and psychologically tempering her enthusiasms for 'radical' modernism or agonistically testing herself against her heroes. Her writings, like those of Barthes, make up a complex intellectual autobiography. Viewing her writings as a 'project' – an ongoing effort to delineate 'what it means to be modern' in both individual and cultural terms – she has made this a very personal pursuit. She often seems to be quarrelling with herself and there is certainly a narcissism in her efforts to act as a 'theorist of [her] own sensibility'. But this is also a strength of her work as she has made of this self-analysis a mode of general cultural inquiry.

Sontag's self-cultivation assumes a privileged modernist birthright. In this she mimics her New York predecessors, for as Daniel Bell has observed of the mid-century intellectuals, 'We thought that we would be the heirs of sensibility, the heirs, in effect, of what the *modern* was all about.'[6] We need to add to this Irving Howe's emphasis that the: 'New York writers came at the end of the modernist experience … One shorthand way of describing their situation, a cause of both their feverish brilliance and their recurrent instability, is to say that *they came late*.'[7] One short hand way of describing Sontag's situation is to say that she came even later. She established herself as a New York intellectual and a modernist at a time when both these entitlements to cultural vanguardism were losing authority. Like many of her predecessors she embraced modernism as a form of utopian compensation, a way of making herself at home in a cosmopolitan intellectual culture, while identifying with the 'feeling of homelessness' (*AI* 69) she believed distinguished the restlessness and alienation of the modern intellectual. Such identifications, as she often implies, have a 'posthumous' quality. While she brought new energy and insights to New York intellectual criticism she very soon began to define herself as an epilogist of high modernism, allegorising her own melancholy responses to the sense of an ending she associated with the eschatology of modernity.

Today, Sontag is widely viewed as something of an eccentric in American intellectual life and one of 'the last intellectuals' of the New York tradition.[8] Her commitment to the role of the free-floating generalist and her sense of a common culture responsive to rational thought and argument can seem anachronistic given the fragmentation of coherent political and cultural publics in the United States in the last thirty years. Thomas Bender argues that the intellectual can no longer assume a public:

> There are now a plurality of audiences within a public culture that is essentially cosmopolitan and contested. In the past a fragment of the public, the educated middle-class audience … was able to pose with success as the whole. Today, the public is at once increasingly representative, and more fragmented, making it harder to find, to reach, and to define. The intellectual no longer has an unselfconscious 'we' relationship to the public.[9]

In place of a common culture there is a plurality of cultures and tastes and the intellectual's address to a public is accordingly provisional and circumscribed. Generalism has no special claim under these conditions; indeed, as Todd Gitlin wryly notes, 'general thought is so distinctive a taste, now, as to qualify as a special interest alongside personal computing, running, and so on at the serious newsstand'.[10]

There is evidence to support Bender's view that as the public sphere becomes increasingly polycentric intellectuals will limit the province of their thinking to localised or specialised contexts. However, the universalising public intellectual has not yet disappeared and many continue to find a large, differentiated audience. Sontag stands as a singular if not a sole example. She is not the last intellectual, but an intellectual who has made public her own ambivalent, speculative, and provocative thoughts on the decline of the new.

NOTES

Introduction

1   William Phillips, 'Radical Styles', *Partisan Review*, XXXVI, 1969, p. 388.

2   Phillips, 'Radical Styles', p. 388.

3   Stanley Aronowitz, 'Opposites Detract: Sontag versus Barthes for Barthes' Sake', *The Village Voice Literary Supplement*, November 1982, p. 13.

4   James Toback, 'Whatever You'd Like Susan Sontag to Think, She Doesn't', *Esquire*, July 1968, p. 60.

5   Richard Bernstein, 'Susan Sontag, as Image and as Herself', *New York Times*, 26 January 1989, p. C17.

6   Bernstein, 'Susan Sontag', p. C17.

7   Greil Marcus, 'Paper Tiger', *California Magazine*, January 1983, p. 97.

8   See Monika Beyer, 'A Life Style Is Not a Life: An Interview with Susan Sontag', *Polish Perspectives*, XXIII, IX, 1980, p. 43.

9   Susan Sontag, 'Preface' to Roland Barthes, *Writing Degree Zero*, Boston, 1970, p. xi.

10 Alvin Gouldner, *The Future of Intellectuals and the Rise of the New Class*, New York, 1979, p. 33.

11 Jonathan Cott, 'Susan Sontag: The Rolling Stone Interview', *Rolling Stone*, 4 October 1979, p. 53.

12 Susan Sontag, 'Pilgrimage', *The New Yorker*, 21 December 1987, pp. 38-54.

13 Sontag, 'Pilgrimage', p. 42.

14 Sontag, 'Pilgrimage', p. 40.

15 Roger Copeland, 'The Habits of Consciousness', *Commonweal*, 13 February 1981, p. 87.

16 Cott, 'Susan Sontag', p. 52.

17 William Cain, 'An Interview with Irving Howe', *American Literary History*, I, autumn 1989, p. 561.

18 Irving Howe, 'The New York Intellectuals', *Decline of the New*, London, 1971, pp. 240-1.

19 Daniel Bell, 'The "Intelligentsia" in American Society', *Sociological Journeys: Essays 1960-1980*, London, 1980, p. 131.

20 Harold Rosenberg, *The Tradition of the New*, London, 1970, p. 10.

21 Howe, *Decline of the New*, p. vii.

22 On the New Class, see Gouldner, *The Future of Intellectuals and the Rise of the New Class*; Barbara and John Ehrenreich, 'The Professional–Managerial Class', in *Between Labour and Capital*, ed. Pat Walker, Boston, 1979; Andrew Ross, *No Respect: Intellectuals and Popular Culture*, New York and London, 1989, Chapter Seven.

23 Lionel Trilling, *The Liberal Imagination*, London, 1961, p. vv.

24 Wayne Koestenbaum, 'Immunities', *The Yale Review*, LXXX 1989, p. 466.

25 The only book-length study is Sohnya Sayres, *Susan Sontag: The Elegiac Modernist*, New York and London, 1990.

26 Tom Shone, 'Side by Side by Sontag', *Sunday Times Magazine*, 2 August 1992, p. 45.

27 Angela McRobbie, 'The Modernist Style of Susan Sontag', *Feminist Review*, XXXXVIII, summer 1991, p. 7.

28 McRobbie, 'The Modernist Style', pp. 5, 7, 18.

29 McRobbie, 'The Modernist Style', p. 4.

30 McRobbie, 'The Modernist Style', p. 2.

31 This symbolic role was applied early to Sontag. In his review of *Against Interpretation* Burton Feldman wrote: 'Miss Sontag is the latest heir and perhaps leading example today of that strenuously intellectual woman starting with Margaret Fuller and coming forward to Mary McCarthy. She shares with these a quick mind, a good education, a high-handed manner, and an inability to stop nagging.' Burton Feldman, 'Evangelist of the New', *Denver Quarterly*, spring 1966, p. 152. Within the New York intellectual world it was Norman Podhoretz who most explicitly identified Sontag with the 'Dark Lady' role. Commenting on the rapidity of her rise to prominence he suggests this

> must be attributed to the coincidental availability of a vacant position in the culture. That position … was Dark Lady of American Letters, a position that had originally been carved out by Mary McCarthy in the 'thirties and 'forties. But Miss McCarthy no

longer occupied it, having been recently promoted to the more dig-
nified status of *Grande Dame* as a reward for her long years of
brilliant service. The next Dark Lady would have to be, like her,
clever, learned, good-looking, capable of writing family-type criticism as well as fiction with a strong trace of naughtiness ... a public
existed when [Sontag] arrived on the scene which was searching for
a new Dark Lady, and she was so obviously right that a spontane-
ous decision was made on all sides to cast her for the role.

Norman Podhoretz, *Making It*, London, 1968, pp. 154-5.

32　I follow Sontag on Paul Goodman: 'His so-called amateurism is identical with his genius: that amateurism enabled him to bring to the
questions of schooling, psychiatry, and citizenship an extraordinary,
curmudgeonly accuracy of insight and freedom to envisage practical
change' (*USS* 8).

Chapter 1

1　Irving Howe, 'The New York Intellectuals', *Decline of the New*,
London, 1971, pp. 248, 258.

2　James Gilbert, *Writers and Partisans: A History of Literary Radical-
ism in America*, New York, 1968, p. 205. See also Terry A. Cooney,
The Rise of the New York Intellectuals: Partisan Review and its Circle,
Madison, 1986.

3　'Our Country and Our Culture', *Partisan Review*, XIX, May–June
1952.

4　Howe, *Decline of the New*, p. 224.

5　Clement Greenberg, 'Avant-Garde and Kitsch', *Art and Culture*,
Boston, 1961, pp. 5-7.

6　Dwight Macdonald, 'Masscult and Midcult', *Against the American
Grain: Essays on the Effects of Mass Culture*, New York, 1983, pp. 3-
75. Other relevant essays by Macdonald include 'A Theory of Popular
Culture', *Politics*, I, February 1944, pp. 20-3 and 'A Theory of Mass
Culture', in *Mass Culture: The Popular Arts in America*, ed. Bernard
Rosenberg and David Manning White, New York, 1957, pp. 59-73. In
the early 1950s Philip Rahv expressed a similar desire to distance an
elite intellectual culture from mass culture: ' if under present conditions we cannot stop the ruthless expansion of mass culture, the least
we can do is to keep apart and refuse its favours'. Philip Rahv, *Literature and the Sixth Sense*, Boston, 1970, p. 182. It has been noted that
there is a rhetoric of 'contamination' evident in the postwar writings
on mass culture by many New York intellectuals. On Cold War connotations of this rhetoric, see Andrew Ross, *No Respect: Intellectuals
and Popular Culture*, New York and London, 1989, Chapter 2. For a
critical summary of the mass culture debate, see Christopher

Brookeman, *American Culture and Society Since the 1930s*, London, 1984, pp. 41-58.

7   Harold Rosenberg was something of an exception, identifying the paradoxes and politics of 'the tradition of the new', and bitterly attacking the commercial and uncritical practices of 'the taste bureaucracies of modern art'. See Harold Rosenberg, *The Tradition of the New*, London, 1970.

8   Lionel Trilling, *The Liberal Imagination*, London, 1961, p. xv.

9   Thomas Bender, *New York Intellect: A History of Intellectual Life in New York City, From 1750 to the Beginnings of Our Own Time*, Baltimore, 1988, p. 256.

10 Howe, 'The New York Intellectuals', p. 253.

11 See Herbert Marcuse, *Eros and Civilisation*, New York, 1962, first published 1955; Norman O. Brown, *Life Against Death: The Psychoanalytical Meaning of History*, Middletown, Conn., 1985, first published 1959.

12 Richard Chase, 'The Fate of the Avant-Garde', *Partisan Review*, XXIV, summer 1957, pp. 363-75.

13 See Susan Sontag, 'Non-Writing and the Art Scene', in *The New Art*, ed. Gregory Battock, New York, 1973, pp. 152-60.

14 Clement Greenberg, 'Sculpture in Our Time', *Arts Magazine*, June 1958, p. 22.

15 This position is upheld throughout the essays collected in *Art and Culture*.

16 Michael Fried, 'Art and Objecthood', *Artforum*, V, summer 1967, p. 21.

17 Walter Benjamin, 'Surrealism: The Last Snapshot of the European Intelligentsia', in *One Way Sreet and Other Writings*, ed. Susan Sontag, London, 1979, p. 226.

18 See Walter Benjamin, 'The Work of Art in the Age of Mechanical Reproduction', in *Illuminations*, ed. Hannah Arendt, London, 1973, pp. 219-54.

19 Clement Greenberg, 'Surrealist Painting', *The Nation*, 12 August 1944, p. 192.

20 Benjamin, 'The Work of Art', p. 225.

21 John Simon, in a letter to *Partisan Review*, complained: 'All this "camping" serves the purpose of confusing aesthetic as well as moral issues, by ultimately making the good indistinguishable from the bad, the purposive submerged in the sterile, backwards as good as forwards.' 'Two Camps', *Partisan Review*, XXXII, winter 1965, p. 156.

22 Howe, *Decline of the New*, p. 8.

23 Lionel Trilling, 'On the Teaching of Modern Literature', *Beyond Culture*, Oxford, 1980, pp. xii-xiii, 10-26.

24 See Jacques Lacan, *The Language of the Self: The Function of Language in Psychoanalysis*, trans. Anthony Wilden, Baltimore, 1968.

25 Herbert Marcuse, for example, defines art as a 'non-conceptual truth of the senses'. Marcuse, *Eros and Civilisation*, p. 169. In the 1960s many writers conjoined this formalism with political perspectives. For an insightful critique of this practice, see Gerald Graff, 'The Politics of Anti-Realism', *Literature Against Itself: Literary Ideas in Modern Society*, Chicago, 1979, pp. 63-101.

26 See William Phillips, *A Sense of the Present*, New York, 1967, pp. 3-11, 30-43; Howe, *Decline of the New*, 252-4; Rahv, *Literature and the Sixth Sense*, pp. 409-21.

27 Trilling, *Beyond Culture*, p. 179. Irving Howe was also concerned for liberal humanist values, and he believed the new sensibility threatened to undermine 'liberalism as a cast of mind, a structure of norms by means of which to humanise public life. For those of us who have lived through the age of totalitarianism and experienced the débâcle of socialism, this conflict over liberal values is extremely painful.' Howe, *Decline of the New*, p. 249.

28 Richard Gilman, 'Susan Sontag and the Question of the New', *The Confusion of Realms*, London, 1970, p. 38.

29 Robert Mazzocco, 'Swingtime', *New York Review of Books*, 9 June 1966, p. 22.

30 Benjamin DeMott, 'Lady on the Scene', *New York Times Book Review*, 23 January 1966, p. 5.

31 Gilman, 'Susan Sontag', p. 35.

32 Susan Sontag, *Against Interpretation*, New York, 1978, p. viii.

33 Howe, *Decline of the New*, p. 255.

Chapter 2

1 Mark C. Taylor, *Deconstruction in Context: Literature and Philosophy*, Chicago, 1986, p. 3.

2 E. M. Cioran, *The Temptation to Exist*, Chicago, 1968, pp. 138-9.

3 Theodor Adorno, *Aesthetic Theory*, London, 1984, p. 5.

4 Georges Bataille, *Death and Sensuality: A Study of Eroticism and the Taboo*, New York, 1977, pp. 168-70.

5 Fredric Jameson, 'Pleasure: A Political Issue', in *Formations of Pleasure*, London, 1983, p. 14.

6 William Phillips has suggested Sontag's essay 'legitimises a repressed faculty'. William Phillips, 'Radical Styles', *Partisan Review*, XXXVI, 1969, pp. 388-400.

7 Hannah Arendt, *Men in Dark Times*, Harmondsworth, 1973, p. 8.

8   Tony Tanner, *City of Words: American Fiction 1950-1970*, London, 1976, p. 144.

9   Walter Benjamin, 'The Storyteller', in *Illuminations*, ed. Hannah Arendt, London, 1973, p. 94.

10 Peter Brooks, *Reading for the Plot: Design and Intention in Narrative*, Oxford, 1984, p. 95.

11 The morbidity of *Death Kit* is an extreme version of the melancholia many of Sontag's fictional characters evidence. She has also commented, in a 1975 interview, on 'a long-term fascination with mortuary sculpture, architecture, inscriptions, and other such wistful lore that eventually found an unsystematic place in *Death Kit*' (*SSR* 339).

12 Susan Sontag, 'The Role of the Writer as Critic', *Publishers Weekly*, 28 March 1966, pp. 36-7.

13 James Toback, 'Whatever You'd Like Susan Sontag to Think, She Doesn't', *Esquire*, July 1968, p. 60.

14 Frances Fitzgerald, 'A Nice Place to Visit', *New York Review of Books*, 13 March 1969, pp. 28-31.

15 Lawrence M. Bensky, 'Susan Sontag, Indignant, Stoical, Complex, Useful – and Moral', *New York Times Book Review*, 13 July 1969, p. 5.

16 Toback, 'Whatever You'd Like', p. 60.

17 Norman Mailer, *The Armies of the Night*, New York, 1968, pp. 109, 103.

18 'Narcissus', Edward Said reminds us, 'is an ideologue of imperialism'. See Edward Said, *Orientalism*, New York, 1978, Chapter 1.

19 Susan Sontag, 'Some Thoughts on the Right Way (For Us) to Love the Cuban Revolution', *Ramparts*, April 1969, p. 10.

20 Sontag, 'Some Thoughts', pp. 10, 19.

21 Sontag, 'Some Thoughts', p. 18.

22 Sontag, 'Some Thoughts', p. 10.

23 Richard Poirier, *The Aesthetics of Contemporary American Radicalism*, Leicester, 1972, pp. 18-19, 21.

24 Poirier, *The Aesthetics*, pp. 16-17.

25 Sontag, 'Some Thoughts', p. 19.

Chapter 3

1   *Duet for Cannibals*, written and directed by Sontag, Sandrew Film and Theatre (AB) Sweden, 1969. Black and white, 105 minutes. *Brother Carl*, written and directed by Sontag, Sandrew Film and Theatre (AB) Sweden, 1971. Black and white, 97 minutes.

2   Charles Ruas, *Conversations With American Writers*, London, 1984, p. 185.

3   Elizabeth Hardwick, 'Domestic Manners', *Daedalus*, winter 1978, p. 1.

4   See George Levine, 'Our Culture and Our Convictions', *Partisan Review*, XXXIX, 1972, pp. 63-79; Philip Rieff, *The Triumph of the Therapeutic: Uses of Faith after Freud*, New York, 1966; Christopher Lasch, *The Culture of Narcissism*, New York, 1979; Daniel Bell, *The Cultural Contradictions of Capitalism*, New York, 1976.

5   Leo Braudy, 'A Genealogy of Mind', *The New Republic*, 29 November 1980, pp. 43-6.

6   In his review of *Under the Sign of Saturn* David Craven argues that Sontag makes a 'hackneyed effort to turn Benjamin into a delicately apolitical and eccentric intellectual ... Sontag has, with the help of liberal humanists like Hannah Arendt and George Steiner, recrowned Benjamin with [a] belletristic nimbus, thus making him safe for the Academy and for further cultural appropriation.' Craven's review appears in *Telos*, XLVIII, summer 1981, pp. 189-94.

7   Roger Copeland, 'The Habits of Consciousness', *Commonweal*, 13 February 1981, p. 84.

8   For a lucid commentary on these elements of modern essay writing, see Graham Good, *Observing the Self: Studies on the Essay*, London, 1987, Chapter 1.

9   Leo Braudy draws attention to this in his review. Braudy, 'Genealogy', p. 45.

10 Eric L. Santner, *Stranded Objects: Mourning, Memory, and Film in Postwar Germany*, Ithaca and London, 1990, p. 7.

11 Peter Hujar, *Portraits in Life and Death*, New York, 1976.

12 James Alinder, 'An Interview with Susan Sontag', *Untitled*, XIV, 1978, p. 37.

13 William Gass, 'A Different Kind of Art', *New York Times Book Review*, 18 December 1977, p. 30.

14 Gass, 'A Different Kind', p. 30.

15 In a 1981 interview Sontag comments on her peculiar conception of Surrealism. 'All of my essays,' she tells Roger Copeland,

> are attempts to ask what it means to be modern, to delineate the modern sensibility from as many different angles as possible.One of the names I've found for this sensibility is surrealism, but I'm aware of the fact that I conceive of surrealism in a very personal way ... In a sense, I suppose I stretched the term surrealism in much the same way I stretched the notion of camp ... Perhaps I latched onto the word surrealism fleeing from notions like camp and kitsch. Better to use a word that people won't get so excited about.

Copeland, 'Habits', p. 84.

16 Paul Brennan, 'Sontag in Greenwich Village: An Interview', *London Magazine*, April–May 1979, pp. 97-8.

17 Editors of *Performing Arts Journal*, 'On Art and Consciousness', *Performing Arts Journal*, II, 1976, p. 32.

18 Walter Benjamin, 'The Work of Art in the Age of Mechanical Reproduction', in *Illuminations*, ed. Hannah Arendt, London, 1973, pp. 226, 236.

19 See Hal Foster, *Recodings: Art, Spectacle, Cultural Politics*, Port Townsend, Washington, 1983, p. 24.

20 Sontag is determined not to acknowledge any direct trafficking between the photograph and a lived experience: *all* photographic seeing is dissociated in her text. John Berger, in a generally favourable review of *On Photography*, questions whether Sontag's views on 'dissociative seeing' always apply:

> There are photographs which belong to private experience and there are those (probably the majority) which are used publicly. The private photograph – the portrait of a mother, a picture of a daughter, a group photo of one's own team – is appreciated and read in a context which is continuous with that from which the camera removed it. It is a momento from the same life being lived. Such a photograph remains surrounded by the very meaning from which it was severed ... The publicly used photograph usually presents the unknown – or, at the most, that which has only become known through other photographs. It offers information of a kind; information severed from experience. It is almost pure code. If the publicly used photograph belongs anywhere, it belongs to the memory of a total stranger.

John Berger, 'Photography: God of the Instant', *Seven Days*, 7 April 1978, pp. 28-30.

21 Christopher Lasch, 'The Narcissistic Personality of Our Time', *Partisan Review*, XLIV, 1977, p. 18.

22 Lasch, 'The Narcisstic Personality', p. 19.

23 Lasch, 'The Narcisstic Personality', p. 18.

24 Such defensive assertion is also evident in a 1978 interview in which she is closely questioned about her specialist knowledge of photography. The interviewer presses her on when and how her interest in photography developed and suggests the 'photography community might question your commitment to the medium'. Sontag's response is that such a complaint shows no understanding of 'what the intellectual is'. *On Photography*, she goes on, 'is not addressed to photography professionals. It is addressed to people who want to think about what is going on in the modern world ... It seems to me the objections of the photographic community must be ultimately objections to some kind of free speculation.' This is an illuminating exchange. The interviewer is sceptical about Sontag's lack of specialist credentials and so formulates the specialist's protective question: on what authority do you write or speak? For Sontag, the authority is self-evident, that of an educated and freely speculative mind ('I started [writing on photo-

graphy] because I think about photographs a lot.') As we have seen, though, her 'free speculation' bespeaks specific cultural, political, and critical values which play a major part in focusing her intellectual concerns and shaping her arguments. Alinder, 'An Interview', p. 35

25 Fredric Jameson, *Postmodernism, or, The Cultural Logic of Late Capitalism*, London, 1991, pp. 1-54.

26 Jameson, *Postmodernism*, p. 48.

27 A subtext of 'Unguided Tour' is its examination of (mass) tourism as a semiotic practice. Jonathan Culler provides some pertinent commentary on 'the semiotics of tourism', suggesting that 'tourists are the agents of semiotics – all over the world they are engaged in reading cities, landscapes and cultures as sign systems'. This is to say that tourism exemplifies in exaggerated form the domination of signification over use value, where all objects can only be recognised through signifying structures that 'mark' them. Tourists, Culler notes, 'set out in quest of the authentic' but 'the authentic is not someting unmarked or undifferentiated; authenticity is a sign relation'. Jonathan Culler, 'The Semiotics of Tourism', *Framing the Sign: Criticism and Its Institutions*, Oxford, 1988, pp. 158-61.

28 Theodor Adorno, *Minima Moralia: Reflections from Damaged Life*, London, 1979, p. 37.

Chapter 4

1 Charles Ruas, *Conversations With American Writers*, London, 1984, p. 187.

2 See, for example, 'The Salmagundi Interview', (*SSR* 335-6).

3 'Poland and Other Questions: Communism and the Left', *The Nation*, 27 February 1982, pp. 230-1. The authorised transcript of Sontag's address is published under this title along with several responses and a 'Reply' by Sontag, pp. 229-8.

4 See 'Poland and Other Questions', pp. 231-7; Leon Weseltier, 'Ideas in Season', *Partisan Review*, XLIX, 1982, pp. 420-8; Richard Grenier, 'The Conversion of Susan Sontag', *The New Republic*, 14 April 1982, pp. 15-19.

5 'Poland and Other Questions', p. 232.

6 For a detailed reading of this issue, see Robert J. Barnham, 'Speaking Itself: Susan Sontag's Town Hall Address', *The Quarterly Journal of Speech*, August 1989, pp. 259-76.

7 See Andrew Kopkind, 'The Return of Cold War Liberalism', in *The Nation 1865-1990*, ed. Katrina Vanden Heuvel, London, 1990, pp. 332-41.

8 'Poland and Other Questions', p. 238.

9   Eileen Manion and Sherry Simon, 'An Interview with Susan Sontag', *Canadian Journal of Political and Social Theory*, winter 1985, p. 11.

10 Manion and Simon, 'An Interview', p. 11.

11 Hilton Kramer, 'Anti-communism and the Sontag Circle', *The New Criterion*, September 1986, pp. 6-7.

12 Manion and Simon, 'An Interview', p. 9.

13 William Phillips, '*Partisan Review* Then and Now', *Partisan Review*, LI, 1984, p. 491.

14 Daniel Bell, 'Our Country: 1984', *Partisan Review*, LI, 1984, p. 632.

15 See James Atlas, 'Intellectuals on the Right', *Dialogue*, III 1986, p. 40-5.

16 There are many texts dealing with the 'theory revolution' in the humanities. See, for example, William Cain, *The Crisis in Criticism: Theory, Literature and Reform in English Studies*, Baltimore, 1984; Gerald Graff, *Professing Literature: An Institutional History*, Chicago, 1987.

17 Manion and Simon, 'An Interview', p. 13.

18 Sontag has written about her involvement in the international conference scene. See 'When Writers Talk Among Themselves', *New York Times Book Review*, 5 January 1986, pp. 1, 22-3.

19 Per Wastberg, 'Moral Authority', in *The Writer and Human Rights*, ed. Toronto Arts Group for Human Rights, Toronto, 1983, p. 229.

20 Wastberg, 'Moral Authority', p. 230.

21 Carl Miller, 'Interpreting AIDS', *City Limits*, 30 March–6 April 1989, p. 17.

22 Jonathan Cott, 'Susan Sontag: The Rolling Stone Interview', *Rolling Stone*, 4 October 1979, p. 49.

23 Michael Ignatieff, 'Modern Dying', *The New Republic*, 26 December 1988, p. 29.

24 Richard Goldstein, 'Bishop Berkeley's Virus', *The Village Voice*, 14 March 1989, p. 50.

25 D. A. Miller, 'Sontag's Urbanity', *October*, 1989, p. 94.

26 Miller, 'Sontag's Urbanity', p. 92.

27 Wayne Koestenbaum, 'Immunities', *The Yale Review*, LXXX, 1990, pp. 446, 471.

28 Susan Sontag, 'The Way We Live Now', *The New Yorker*, 18 August 1986, pp. 42-51.

29 Tom Shone, 'Side by Side by Sontag', *Sunday Times Magazine*, 2 August 1992, p. 44.

30 Shone, 'Side by Side', pp. 44-5.

31 Richard Jenkyns, 'Eruptions', *The New Republic*, 7 and 14 September 1992, pp. 48-9. See also Bruce Bawer, 'That Sontag Woman', *The New*

Criterion, September 1992, pp. 30-7.

32 *Face to Face*, BBC Television, 1992.

33 *Face to Face*.

Conclusion

1 John Banville, 'By Lava Possessed', *New York Times Book Review*, 9 August 1992, p. 1.

2 Tom Shone, 'Side by Side by Sontag', *Sunday Times Magazine*, 2 August 1992, p. 45.

3 See Leslie Garis, 'Susan Sontag Finds Romance', *New York Times Magazine*, 2 August 1992, pp. 31, 43.

4 *Alice in Bed: A Play in Eight Scenes*, New York, 1993.

5 Charles Ruas, *Conversations With American Writers*, London, 1984, p. 185.

6 Daniel Bell, 'The "Intelligentsia in American Society', *Sociological Journeys: Essays 1960-1980*, London, 1980, p. 132.

7 Irving Howe, *Decline of the New*, London, 1971, p. 218.

8 See Russell Jacoby, *The Last Intellectuals: American Culture in the Age of Academe*, New York, 1987.

9 Thomas Bender, *Intellect and Public Life: Essays on the Social History of Academic Intellectuals in the United States*, Baltimore and London, 1993, p. 144.

10 Todd Gitlin, 'Sociology for Whom? Criticism for Whom?' in *Sociology in America*, ed. Herbert J. Gans, Los Angeles, 1990, p. 222.

INDEX

enlightened ideals of, 12, 102, 115-6, 117

moral inquiry, writing as, 11, 108-9, 113, 117-18

negation, 10-11, 40, 50, 54,73, 98-9, 118

neoconservatism, 102, 104, 106, 107, 108, 109, 115, 116, 117

New Class, 12

The New Criterion, 106

New Critics, 9, 41

New Left, 71, 73, 102

new sensibility, 2, 16-17, 20-3, 26, 43, 72

New York intellectuals, 7-9, 12, 15, 16-27, 34, 35, 42, 44-5, 62, 73, 75, 96, 103-4, 106-8, 128-9

New York Review of Books, 44, 63, 88

New York Times Book Review, 44

New Yorker, 109

Old Left, 71, 73, 102

Paris, 7, 37, 74, 77

Partisan Review, 1, 6, 7, 18, 19, 34, 62, 106

passion, intellect and, 10, 123, 126, 127, 128

pathos, 80, 98

Pavese, Cesare, 37

PEN, 13, 108-9

PEN American centre, 102

Phillips, William, 1, 106

photography, 4, 11; *see also On Photography*

pluralism, 92, 95, 96, 98

Podhoretz, Norman, 107

Polish Solidarity movement, 103

Pop Art, 25, 49

pornographic literature, 4, 31; *see also* 'The Pornographic Imagination'

postmodern, 44, 75, 86, 87, 98, 116, 119

psychoanalysis, 31, 39

public intellectual, 12, 62, 107-8, 109, 129

public persona, Sontag's, 1-3, 105-6

Rahv, Philip, 18

reason, 15, 105, 116-17

revolution, 68-9, 71-2, 105, 120, 122

Riefenstahl, Leni, 76, 82-6

Rieff, David, 7

Rieff, Philip, 7

Rosenberg, Harold, 4, 8, 96

The Tradition of the New, 9

Sade, Marquis de, 40, 51

Sarraute, Nathalie, 10, 28

Sartre, Jean Paul, 37, 55

silence, 10, 38, 46-55, 57, 60, 69, 70, 73, 105, 118, 122

Sixties (1960s), 2, 75, 106, 115

Smith, Jack, 34, 41

Smith, W. Eugene, 89,

Sontag, Susan

    Against Interpretation, 2, 16-45, 48, 51, 54, 61, 69, 77, 93

    'Against Interpretation', 21-6, 28, 46

    AIDS and Its Metaphors, 101, 105, 110, 114-18

    Alice in Bed, 127

    The Benefactor, 37-40, 55, 61, 101

    Death Kit, 47, 54-61, 70, 78, 101

    Illness as Metaphor, 101, 105, 110-13, 114, 116, 118, 123

    'Notes on Camp', 22, 33-5

    'Old Complaints Revisited', 105

    On Photography, 26, 75, 88-99, 105, 113, 121, 123

    'Pilgrimage', 5-6, 126

    'The Pornographic Imagination', 51-4, 58, 72

    'The Role of the Writer as Critic', 61-2

    'Some Thoughts on the Right Way (for us) to Love the Cuban Revolution', 71

    Styles of Radical Will, 46-54, 63, 70, 77, 78, 98

    A Susan Sontag Reader, 101

    'Trip to Hanoi', 46, 54, 61-73, 105